ISOBEL ARMSTRONG
Consultant Editor

G. K. CHESTERTON

G. K. CHESTERTON

Michael D. Hurley

NORTHCOTE
BRITISH COUNCIL

© Copyright 2012 by Michael D. Hurley

First published by Northcote House Publishers Ltd, Horndon House, Horndon, Tavistock, Devon, PL19 9NQ, United Kingdom.
Tel: +44 (0) 1822 810066 Fax: +44 (0) 1822 810034.

British Library Cataloguing-in-Publication Data
A catalogue record for this book is available from the British Library

ISBN 978-0-7463-1210-0 hardcover
ISBN 978-0-7463-1211-7 paperback

Typeset by PDQ Typesetting, Newcastle-under-Lyme
Printed and bound in the United Kingdom

To Natasha, Francesca and Clemmie

What was wonderful about childhood is that anything in it was a wonder. It was not merely a world full of miracles; it was a miraculous world.
G. K. Chesterton, *Autobiography* (1936)

Contents

Biographical Outline

1874   Gilbert Keith Chesterton is born on 29 May (Campden Hill, London).

1887   Enrols as a day student at St Paul's School.

1892   Enters the Slade School of Art, and also takes literature classes at University College London. A period of religious uncertainty and self-described 'lunacy'.

1895   Leaves the Slade without a degree. Works as a sub-editor for two publishing firms; reviews books; also contributes poems and articles to several journals.

1896   Meets his future wife, Frances Blogg.

1899   Leaves publishing firms to concentrate efforts on journalism and writing.

1900   Meets Hilaire Belloc. Publically opposes the Boer War in *The Speaker*. Publishes his first books: *Greybeards at Play*; *The Wild Knight*.

1901   Marries Frances Blogg. Publication of *The Defendant*.

1902   Publication of *Twelve Types*.

1903   Publication of *Robert Browning*. Begins a regular Saturday column for the *Daily News*.

1904   Declines Chair of Literature at Birmingham University; meets Father John O'Connor (the inspiration for Father Brown). Publication of *G. F. Watts*; *The Napoleon of Notting Hill*.

1905   Becomes a columnist for the *Illustrated London News*. Publiation of *The Club of Queer Trades*; *Heretics*.

1906   Publication of *Charles Dickens*.

1908   Publication of *The Man Who Was Thursday*; *All Things Considered*; *Orthodoxy*.

1909   Publication of *George Bernard Shaw*; *Tremendous Trifles*; *The Ball and the Cross*.

1910   Moves from London to Beaconsfield. Publication of *What's Wrong With the World*; *Alarms and Discursions*; *William Blake*; serialization of *The Innocence of Father Brown*.

1911   Belloc begins the *Eye-Witness* (later the *New Witness*), to which Chesterton contributes. Publication of *Appreciations and Criticisms of the Works of Charles Dickens*; *The Innocence of Father Brown*; *The Ballad of the White Horse*.

1912   The *New Witness* is founded, with Cecil Chesterton as editor until 1916. Publication of *Manalive*; *A Miscellany of Men*.

1913   Leaves the *Daily News* for the *Daily Herald*. The Marconi affair. Chesterton ends association with the *Daily News*. His brother, Cecil, becomes a Catholic. Publication of *The Victorian Age in Literature*; *Magic*.

1914   Falls seriously ill from an oedema; reportedly in a coma for several months from late in the year; markedly better by March. Publication of *The Flying Inn*; *The Wisdom of Father Brown*; *The Barbarism of Berlin*.

1915   Convalesces till June. Publication of *Letters to an Old Garibaldian*; *Poems*; *The Crimes of England*.

1916   Becomes editor of the *New Witness*.

1917   Publication of *A Short History of England*; *Utopia of Usurers*.

1918   Cecil dies at war, in France. Visits Ireland.

1919   Sets out on trip to Palestine and Rome in late December. Publication of *Irish Impressions*.

1920   Publication of *The Superstition of Divorce*; *The New Jerusalem*; *The Uses of Diversity*.

1921   Lecture trip to America (Jan–April).

1922   Chesterton's father, Edward, dies. Received into the Catholic Church on 30 July, aged forty-eight. Publication of *Eugenics and other Evils*; *What I Saw in America*; *The Man Who Knew Too Much*; *The Ballad of St Barbara*.

1923   *The New Witness* folds. Publication of *Fancies versus Fads*; *St Francis of Assisi*.

1925   Launches *G.K.'s Weekly*. Publication of *The Superstitions of the Sceptic*; *Tales of the Long Bow*; *The Everlasting Man*; *William Cobbett*; *Collected Poems*.

1926   The Distributist League is founded. Publication of *The Incredulity of Father Brown*; *The Outline of Sanity*; *The*

Queen of Seven Swords; The Catholic Church and Conversion.

1927   Visits Poland. Broadcast debate with Bernard Shaw (later published as *Do We Agree?*). Publication of *The Return of Don Quixote; The Secret of Father Brown; The Judgement of Dr Johnson; Robert Louis Stevenson.*

1928   Publication of *Generally Speaking.*

1929   Visits Rome. Publication of *The Poet and the Lunatics; The Thing; G.K.C as M.C.*

1930   Publication of *Four Faultless Felons; The Resurrection of Rome; Come to Think of It.* Visits America for the second time. Lectures at the University of Notre Dame.

1931   Publication of *All is Grist.*

1932   Begins series of radio talks on BBC. Publication of *Chaucer; Sidelights on New London and Newer York; Christendom in Dublin.*

1933   His mother, Marie, dies. Publication of *All I Survey; St Thomas Aquinas.*

1934   Visits Rome, Sicily and Malta. Made Knight Commander with Star, Order of St Gregory the Great. Publication of *Avowals and Denials.*

1935   Visits France, Spain and Italy. Publication of *The Scandal of Father Brown; The Well and the Shallows.*

1936   Visits Lourdes, and Lisieux. Dies on 14 June (Beaconsfield, London). Publication of *As I Was Saying; Autobiography.*

1937   Publication of *The Paradoxes of Mr Pond.*

1938   His widow, Frances, dies.

Preface

This book differs from standard accounts of Chesterton in that it does not focus on his thinking or his writing style but attempts instead to consider both of these together; specifically, it considers the relationship between the two. There have been a number of subtle and scrupulously researched accounts of his philosophy, his theology and his political views; as there have been ample admirable studies of his fiction, his poetry and his other literary writings. But what there has not been – and what this present book aims to provide – is a sustained examination of how he thinks *through* language, in ways that confound attempts to read him as a thinker without first appreciating him as a writer.

This book is untypical also in its methodology. There is no linear narrative; Chesterton's diverse writings are taken in separate chapters designed to inform and correct each other, to show how different genres of his writing allow and encourage the expression of different kinds of thinking.

I am most grateful to Robin Kirkpatrick, Robert Macfarlane, Malcolm Guite and Peter Hardwick for the intelligence and sympathetic scepticism with which they read drafts of this book. Geir Hasnes's expertise, bibliographic and biographical, was freely given and extremely valuable. Finally, I would like to thank the Warden and Fellows of Robinson College, Cambridge, for supporting my research. This book is dedicated to my children, but has only been made possible by the loving encouragement of my wife.

Cambridge,
August 2011

Abbreviations and References

This book argues through (and with) Chesterton's own words. For this reason the text is thick with quotations, most of which are woven into the syntax of the argument. It has therefore been necessary to use a large number of abbreviations for frequently cited material. Where possible, quotations are taken from his *Collected Works* (Ignatius Press) and given the in-text reference *CW* (followed by volume and page number). At the time of going to press, a number of his works have yet to be published in the *Collected Works*, or, in the case of his poems and essays, only partly published. All quotations from his poems have therefore been taken from *The Collected Poems of G. K. Chesterton* (London: Methuen & Co., 1958 [1933]), and abbreviated in-text as *CP*. Quotations have been drawn from the following collections of his essays:

AC	*All Things Considered* (London: Methuen & Co., 1908)
AD	*Alarms and Discursions* (London: Methuen & Co., 1910)
AG	*All is Grist* (London: Methuen & Co., 1931)
AS	*All I Survey* (London: Methuen & Co., 1933)
AW	*As I Was Saying* (London: Methuen & Co, 1936)
CI	*Come to Think of It* (London: Methuen & Co., 1930)
FF	*Fancies Versus Fads* (London: Methuen & Co., 1923)
GC	*G. K. C. As M. C.* (London: Methuen & Co., 1929)
GS	*Generally Speaking* (London: Methuen & Co., 1928)
MM	*A Miscellany of Men* (London: Methuen & Co., 1912)
TD	*The Defendant* (London: Brimley Johnson, 1901)
TT	*Tremendous Trifles* (London: Methuen & Co., 1909)

Other frequently cited works not yet published in the *Collected Works* include:

BS   *George Bernard Shaw* (London: C. Tingling & Co., 1949)
GW   *G. F. Watts* (London: Duckworth & Co., 1920)
PL   *The Poet and the Lunatics* (Yorkshire: House of Stratus, 2001)
PP   *The Paradoxes of Mr Pond* (London: House of Stratus, 2001)
RB   *Robert Browning* (London: Macmillan & Co., 1903)
WB   *William Blake* (London: Duckworth & Co., 1920)
WC   *William Cobbett* (London: Hodder and Stoughton, 1925)

These frequently cited works of secondary criticism have also been given in-text abbreviated references:

CJ   *G. K. Chesterton: The Critical Judgements, 1900–1937* ed. D. J. Conlon (Antwerp: Antwerp Studies in English Literature, 1976)
HC   *G. K. Chesterton: A Half Century of Views* ed. D. J. Conlon (Oxford: Oxford University Press, 1987)
PC   *Hugh Kenner, Paradox in Chesterton* (London: Sheed & Ward, 1948)

Introduction

A man publishes a series of poems, vigorous, perplexing, and unique. The critics read them, and they decide that he has failed as a poet, but that he is a remarkable philosopher and logician. They then proceed to examine his philosophy, and show with great triumph that it is unphilosophical, and to examine his logic and show with great triumph that it is not logical... (*RB* 133)

Six foot four, and twenty-one stone; wearing a cape and carrying a swordstick, or a loaded revolver: G. K. Chesterton was a hard man to ignore. And not only in person; in print, he was if anything more daunting and improbable. He bestrode a dozen genres. Novelist, essayist, biographer, poet, playwright, historian, journalist, Christian apologist, literary and social critic: he produced thousands of essays, hundreds of poems and short stories, around eighty books and several plays. Whatever his contemporaries thought of him, his provoking and prolific energies disallowed indifference. It was not possible not to have an opinion on the man Bernard Shaw called a 'colossal genius'.[1] He was simply too massive.

At his Requiem Mass in Westminster Cathedral on 27 June 1936, Monsignor Ronald Knox declared: 'The man whom we laid to rest the other day in the cemetery at Beaconsfield was one of the greatest men of his time.' Panegyrists are expected to be affectionately extravagant. Knox, though, expressed more than rheumy-eyed nostalgia for a great man departed; his is a clear-sighted vision of a future without that great man. 'If posterity neglects him,' Knox continued, 'it will pronounce judgement not upon him, but upon itself.'[2] These are hard words to read. Knox's proleptic judgement on posterity is a finger pointed at us. For Chesterton has indeed been neglected. Although there are signs that his star may again be in the ascendant, no other

1

figure so loved and influential in the twentieth century is now so little read or discussed in the twenty-first.

Why has he ceased to seem relevant? The question is a perplexing one. Knox emphasized Chesterton's importance 'as a prophet in an age of false prophets',[3] and subsequent biographers have vied in their accounts of how time has told in his favour: from his presages over the Second World War and the rise and fall of Communist Russia, to his foreboding of eugenics and psychiatry (and indeed about man's relationship to science in general). Two of his anxious predictions are recalled with particular piquancy today: that capitalism, especially globalized capitalism, will inevitably expand, and at the expense of individual liberties; and that Mohammed 'created a very big thing, which we have still to deal with'.[4]

But if Chesterton was a 'prophet', it was not as one who boasted divine foresight; he was often not even terribly well informed about the present. When it came to *realpolitik*, he could appear embarrassingly naïve. That was, to some extent, wilful. *What's Wrong With the World* may only be ameliorated, he thought, by the 'unpractical man', and 'inconvenient ideals' (CW 4:42–6;35). 'There is', he believed, 'only one really startling thing to be done with the ideal, and that is to do it' (CW 4:64): 'the huge modern heresy' is of 'altering the human soul to fit its conditions, instead of altering human conditions to fit the human soul' (CW 4:104). The thrilling acuity of his critiques may be explained, then, rather by his innocence than his worldy (or otherworldy) guile. Modish mores, calcified customs, priggishness of all sorts – especially the mincing proprieties of English snobbery – are in this way ingenuously exposed. Just as he understood that fallacies 'do not cease to be fallacies because they become fashions' (CW 35:293), he exemplified how 'The act of defending any of the cardinal virtues has today all the exhilaration of a vice' (TD 7).

This 'innocent' wisdom is expressed as an ability to see the familiar and humdrum as strange and significant. Sherlock Holmes never tires of reminding Watson that 'there is nothing so important as trifles'.[5] Father Brown, Chesterton's clerical detective, has that same Holmesian attention – except that his interest in the 'little things' that are 'infinitely more important' is governed by a very different rationale. Whereas Holmes is

2

scientific, Brown is philosophical; Holmes appeals to logic, Brown, to life. It is precisely his ignorance of detective method and his inability to spot the likely type that grants him his sleuthing power. The first collection of stories bears a deliberate title, *The Innocence of Father Brown*.

'Really simply goluptious' was the verdict of one contemporary reviewer, who signalled the extent to which Chesterton expands the whodunit genre by referring to the collection as 'detective' tales (*CJ* 265). These stories are bursting with speculations that exceed the traditional business of detection. The challenge to the genre does not arise from the irrelevancy of these speculations, however, but from their supposed relevance: philosophy is privileged over facts as a source of insight. Or rather, Father Brown sees facts philosophically. In this sense, more radically than Conan Doyle, Chesterton demonstrates the extent to which a 'trifle' may be nothing of the kind. His energetic denial that 'anything is, or can be, uninteresting' (*TT* 89) insists on seeing the world afresh, even if that means seeing it whimsically; as he explains in the preface to a collection of his essays called – what else? – *Tremendous Trifles*:

> As the reader's eye strays, with hearty relief, from these pages, it probably alights on something, a bed-post or a lamp-post, a window blind or a wall. It is a thousand to one that the reader is looking at something that he has never seen: that is, never realised. He could not write an essay on such a post or wall: he does not know what the post or wall mean.... None of us think enough of these things on which the eye rests. But don't let us let the eye rest. Why should the eye be so lazy? Let us exercise the eye until it learns to see startling facts that run across the landscape as plain as a painted fence. Let us be ocular athletes. Let us learn to write essays on a stray cat or a coloured cloud. I have attempted some such thing in what follows; but anyone else may do it better, if anyone else will only try. (*TT* v–vi)

That parting invitation – 'only try' – teases with terrible possibilities. 'If you look at a thing nine hundred and ninety-nine times,' remarks Auberon Quin in *The Napoleon of Notting Hill*, 'you are perfectly safe; if you look at it the thousandth time, you are in frightful danger of seeing it for the first time.' Quin had been staring at the coat-tails of certain government officials, when, suddenly, he saw the coats' back buttons as the eyes of black dragons:

3

It was only a momentary fancy, but the small clerk found it imbedded in his soul ever afterwards. He never could again think of men in frock-coats except as dragons walking backwards... when first the two black dragons sprang out of the fog upon the small clerk, they had merely the effect of all miracles—they changed the universe. He discovered the fact that all romantics know—that adventures happen on dull days, and not on sunny ones. When the chord of monotony is stretched most tight, then it breaks with a sound like song. (CW 6:227–28)

The fantastic events that follow – Quin is made King of England, and unwittingly incites civil war – all turn on this moment. Momentary fancy is as small as its effects are great: it has 'merely the effect of all miracles'. The universe is changed by the way in which we view it; monotony becomes marvellous; nothing is the same again. *The Napoleon of Notting Hill* was Chesterton's first novel (1904); *The Return of Don Quixote* is his last (1927), and it explores an almost identical story. But the frightfulness, the danger – and, always, the welcome necessity – of seeing the world afresh is a motif that runs throughout his writing. *The Club of Queer Trades* has been described as 'perhaps the least known of Chesterton's many published volumes of short stories'.[6] It happens also to be the volume which reflects most directly his clamant joy. Each *outré* adventure features a character who 'has invented the means by which he earns his living', 'an entirely new trade' that is 'a genuine source of income, the support of its inventor'. We share the protagonist's wonder: 'The discovery of this strange society was a curiously refreshing thing; to realise that there were ten new trades in the world was like looking at the first ship or the first plough. It made a man feel what he should feel, that he was in the childhood of the world' (CW 6:53).

To make a man feel what he should feel, that he was in the childhood of the world. That is the Chestertonian imperative in a sentence. Here (almost at random) is another witness to that impulse, from *The Flying Inn*:

And while he was warring with such words and thoughts, something happened about him and behind him, something he had written about a hundred times and read about a thousand; something he had never seen in his life. It flung faintly across the broad foliage a wan and pearly light far more mysterious than the lost moonshine. It seemed to enter all the doors and windows of the

4

woodland, pale and silent but confident, like men that keep a tryst; soon its white robes had threads of gold and scarlet: and the name of it was morning. (*CW* 7:566)

Warring words give way to mystery, silence, confidence and, ultimately, to a regal, even religious (Hopkinsian), vision of 'gold-vermillion'. Alliteration fetches out delicate but definite rhythms that confer grandeur and purpose. In the first and third sentences this effect is trained across suspended syntax, performing what it describes. A hundred times written; a thousand times read; never before seen: reserving the 'name' of this vision until the very last word, announcing it like an exotic title after a ceremony of subordinate clauses, ensures that we share the character's surprise. For what is revealed is the familiar felt strangely splendid because for the first time viewed with what Ruskin called the artist's 'innocent eye'. He is not 'looking at something that he has never seen', he is looking at something he has 'never realised'.

Viktor Shklovsky coined the term 'defamiliarization' to describe the way literary 'material' is 'obviously created to remove the automatism of perception', where 'the author's purpose is to create the vision which results from that deautomatized perception'.[7] While Chesterton exploits this same literary technique, it is important to note that the 'vision' he creates is not merely literary: it is continuous with the way in which he viewed life. The reason he makes the familiar appear strange in his language is that he saw the world in the same way; and because art opens the possibility of revitalizing our experience of the world. He believed 'about the universal cosmos, or for that matter about every weed and pebble in the cosmos, that men will never rightly realize that it is beautiful, until they realize that it is strange' (*CW* 20:48). 'Poetry is', for him, 'the separation of the soul from some object, whereby we can regard it with wonder' (*CW* 20:49). In his *Autobiography* he looks back at his 'primary problem' that 'grew out of' '[e]very-thing that I have thought and done': 'It was the problem of how men could be made to realize the wonder and splendour of being alive, in environments which their own daily criticism treated as dead-alive, and which their imagination had left for dead' (*CW* 16:132). Repudiating the modernist commonplace that man is metaphysically moribund, he believes in 'a forgotten

5

blaze or burst of astonishment at our own existence' that lurks somewhere 'at the back of our brains' and which it is the 'object of the artistic and spiritual life' to recover: 'to dig for this submerged sunrise of wonder' (CW 16:97).

Notice the common purpose he imagines for 'the artistic and spiritual life' and the daft loveliness with which it is pursued: digging for the sun. Moments like this appear everywhere.[8] Often, they are the structuring conceit of the entire work. *Manalive* tells the story of 'Innocent Smith', whose name (like that of the book in which he appears) speaks for itself. Smith is 'a kind of fanatic of the joy of life'; he 'had somehow made a giant stride from babyhood to manhood, and missed the crisis in youth when most of us grow old' (CW 7:279). But even he must work hard to avoid being 'imprisoned in the commonplace', by strenuously defamiliarizing his existence (CW 7:281). He breaks into his own house to steal his own wine; he has an affair with his own wife. On one consummate occasion, he walks out of his house and all the way around the world that he may arrive where he started and know the place for the first time.

The same trope of the guileless globetrotter is used to explain how Chesterton 'discovered' his faith. *Orthodoxy* begins by asking us to imagine 'a romance about an English yachtsman who slightly miscalculated his course and discovered England under the impression that it was a new island in the South Seas' (CW 1:211). When he goes on to say with 'the heartiest sentiments', 'I am that man in a yacht' (CW 1:213), he is refusing the flippancy implied by his figurative language. He calls the tale a 'romance'; but, for Chesterton, 'the very word "romance" has in it the mystery and ancient meaning of Rome' (CW 1:212). So it is that *The Everlasting Man* opens by describing a story he 'never wrote', conceived as 'a romance of those vast valleys with sloping sides, like those along which the ancient White Horses of Wessex are scrawled along the flanks of the hills' (CW 2:143):

> It concerned some boy whose farm or cottage stood on such a slope, and who went on his travels to find something, such as the effigy and grave of some giant; and when he was far enough from home he looked back and saw that his own farm and kitchen-garden, shining flat on the hill-side like the colours and quarterings of a shield, were but parts of some such gigantic figure, on which he had lived, but which was too large and too close to be seen.[9]

Far from there being a category distinction between the wild adventures of his literary fantasias and his overtly philosophical writing, we may see here how his thinking is itself defined by wildness, adventure, literariness and the fantastical. He warns the reader of *The Everlasting Man* that the spiritual history of the world cannot be told with po-faced pedantry: 'it is necessary to touch the nerve of novelty'. To 'recover the candour and wonder of the child', 'the unspoilt realism and objectivity of innocence', the reader must 'shake off the cloud of mere custom and see the thing as new, if only by seeing it as unnatural': 'We must invoke the most wild and soaring sort of imagination' (*CW* 2:148); the treatment of 'even so serious a subject' requires a style 'deliberately grotesque and fanciful'.[10]

A fine line needs to be respected here. His fiction and his non-fiction cannot be treated identically. His stories are, obviously, to some extent motivated by the exigencies of plot; not everything is philosophically charged. In *The Ball and the Cross*, when the fleeing duelists sail a yacht to what they believe to be the safety of 'an almost unknown rock, lost in the Atlantic' only to find themselves washed up 'on the edge of the Isle of Thanet, a few miles from Margate' (*CW* 7:175), there is no moral to be drawn. It is a bit of plain buffoonery; to treat the event as his 'heartiest sentiments' would be to misread. It is equally obvious, however, that his variations on the theme of the adventurer who sees the familiar for the first time may carry philosophical weight even in his lightest fiction. Consider, for instance, how the Father Brown mystery called 'The Man in the Passage' is solved. Three men witness the prime suspect lurking in a passage. Sir Wilson Seymour reports 'curves and a woman's hair and a man's trousers' (*CW* 12:303). Captain Cutler identifies a 'chimpanzee with humped shoulders and hog's bristles' (*CW* 12:301). In a cute baroque touch, Father Brown meets the devil. But only Father Brown realizes that they have each seen the same person – because the passage contained a mirror. What Father Brown saw may be explained in physical terms: priests wear black and their hats 'have corners just like horns' (*CW* 12:303). What he came to *realize*, though, invites an explanation that is metaphysical. He recognizes himself as a devil because he is so far from being one; he is reflective enough to imagine how his image might be reflected in the world. Sir Wilson

Seymour and Captain Cutler cannot see the world as it really is because they cannot see themselves.

If it may be granted, then, that Chesterton's fiction and his non-fiction overlap in their interests, and that indeed his light style interpenetrates his serious subject matter, how can he be read right? Failure to answer this question adequately is the single greatest reason Chesterton's reputation has sunk over the last century. There have been a number of subtle and scrupulously researched accounts of his writings, from both literary-critical and philosophical perspectives. What there has not been, however – and what this present study aims to provide – is a sustained examination of the ways in which his literary imagination and his philosophical thinking are mutually informing. Scholars have generally emphasized one perspective over – or at the expense of – the other. In this, he especially needs to be defended against his admirers. On the one hand, those who enjoy his verse or his fiction typically cherish its lush quirkiness and epigrammatic swagger as an end in itself. 'A very entertaining evening' is the promise Lucian Gregory extends to Gabriel Syme in *The Man Who Was Thursday*, just before they set out for the secret anarchists' headquarters; and it is this same promise, Kingsley Amis believes, that Chesterton extends to his reader (*HC* 283). To expect more, even of his jolly philosophizing, is to invite disappointment. That the Toby-Jug jester should be taken seriously as a thinker sounds like an unwitting bad joke. Chesterton was painfully aware of the tendency to read his work 'as a piece of poor clowning', as he was at pains to correct this tendency: 'Mere light sophistry is the thing that I happen to despise most of all things, and it is perhaps a wholesome fact that this is the thing of which I am generally accused' (*CW* 1:213).

On the other hand, those who would make the case for him as a thinker generally cannot bring themselves to admire his talent as a writer. 'To judge Chesterton on his "contributions to literature"', writes T. S. Eliot, 'would be to apply the wrong standard of measurement'.[11] The alliterative habit he learnt from Swinburne, the paradoxes and puns he inherited from Wilde, the medievalism he admired in Morris, and indeed the anarchic nursery wisdom he took from Lear: these and other apparently *à la mode* traits are taken for dispensable, *démodé* ornamentation. He is reckoned to be (as James Stephens describes it) 'largely a period talent' (*HC* 65). In short, his thinking is deemed important because it stands apart from its moment, his style is judged too much of that moment to have transcended it. The idea that his writing style may reflect and even inflect his thinking is ignored, or denied. It may be, as Ian Boyd has suggested, that the chief culprits here are those 'professional Catholics' who promote him as an institution and defensively discourage the evaluation of him as a literary artist;[12] but that is by no means the whole story.

In a recent review, A. N. Wilson perhaps says more than he intends and is more right than he knows in praising Hugh Kenner's *Paradox in Chesterton* as the 'most sustained defence of "the intellectual side" of GKC'.[13] Precisely the limitation of Kenner's study (which has no ecclesiastical agenda) is that it only looks at one side of Chesterton: the philosopher is cut away from the poet. Kenner's surgical skill is considerable, but the operation cannot be thought an unqualified success. Wilson's speech-marks round 'the intellectual side' of Chesterton are the bandages that show the scars; they slow the bleeding, but cannot staunch it. He must be taken whole, or you do not have half of him, you have none of him; he is not half-alive, he is dead.

'Chesterton is not so much great because of his published achievement as great because he is right'; 'He is plainly not a great literary artist'; 'His perceptions were metaphysical rather than aesthetic: they never fathered creative fusion.' So begins Kenner's book. He concludes by re-emphasizing the same: 'what must be praised in Chesterton is not the writing but the seeing'; 'The reader who has followed the preceding chapters is well on the way to realizing this fact...' (*PC* 103). *Paradox in Chesterton* carries an introduction by Marshall McLuhan that is equally uncompromising. McLuhan would reverse the growing indifference to Chesterton's 'analogical perception' by welcoming indifference for 'the literary and journalistic Chesterton': 'It is time to abandon' his non-philosophical writing 'to such fate as may await him from future appraisers.' 'In fact,' writes McLuhan, 'it might be the kindest possible service to the essential Chesterton to decry all that part of him which derives so obviously from his time' (*PC* xix).

9

This proposal for the kindest possible service to Chesterton – ostensibly tempered with 'might', but nonetheless presented as 'fact' – continues to be influential. But is it really a 'fact' that to be esteemed as a thinker Chesterton must be abjured as a writer? Or indeed the other way round? 'Throughout Chesterton's work', suggests Kenner, 'the symbol of that central paradox, which Eden established and the Incarnation restored, is laughter: for laughter is the sign of incongruity perceived' (*PC* 93). This is beautifully put, and brilliantly astute; but it is an overly narrow interpretation. There is a wider context for his perception of incongruity that makes sense of both Chesterton the mystic and also Chesterton the phrase-maker. That wider context is 'queerness'.

'Queer' comes from the Scottish, and perhaps the Low German 'quer', meaning 'oblique', 'squint' or 'perverse'; 'query' (like 'inquiry', 'quest' and 'question') comes from the Latin 'quære', meaning 'to ask'. Although there is therefore no etymological link between these like-sounding words, Chesterton presses them into an etiological relationship. In Aristotle's sense, his philosophy 'arises from wonder'; 'astonishment and perplexity' inspires awe, which inspires questioning.[14] In turn, Chesterton inspires the reader to question by presenting the ordinary as extraordinary. To focus exclusively on his achievement as 'the prince of paradox' is to miss his sense of queerness, and his attendant sense of wonder. In the *The Paradoxes of Mr Pond* we are told that 'the stigmata of the stylistic methods of Mr. Pond' – his habit for paradox – is taken by 'the stupid' as something of isolated interest (*PP* 118). Whereas: 'the clever stopped him because they knew that, behind each of these queer compact contradictions, there was a very queer story' (*PP* 42). If we stop to ask what story lies behind Chesterton's queer style, the 'symbol of that central paradox, which Eden established and the Incarnation restored' emerges as part of a more thoroughly pervasive awareness of 'incongruity perceived' than Kenner allows. Chesterton's 'queerness' subsumes the most pressingly strange article of his faith, that God could die, and did for man ('quer' also happens to mean 'cross'); but his imaginative investment in queerness also extends to 'every weed and pebble in the cosmos'.

The connection between Christ's crucifixion and the quotidian contents of 'What I found in my pocket' (*TT* 87–92) is the connexion between Chesterton's metaphysics and his verbalism, his argument and his humour. The anarchic mastermind of *The Man Who Was Thursday* remarks at one point, 'Moderate strength is shown in violence, supreme strength is shown in levity'. The supreme strength of Chesterton's talent shows itself in his ability to think through language by means that outwit the limitations of propositional logic, and which shows itself most clearly in his willingness to delight when he is being most serious. 'I have never understood', he confesses, 'why a solid argument is any less solid because you make the illustrations as entertaining as you can' (CW 16:163); it is a 'sane' man who can have 'tragedy in his heart and comedy in his head' (TT 215). Or as he elsewhere has it: 'About what else than the serious subjects can one possibly make jokes?'[15] Even when it came to his religion, which 'mattered furiously to him',[16] he was playful. For he was always earnest about play; he concludes his essay on 'why grown-up people do not play with toys' with the claim: 'My toy theatre is as philosophical as the drama of Athens' (TT 151).

This confluence of light style with serious subject irrigates even the scholastic aridity of Church history. 'Modern investigators of miraculous history have', Chesterton reports, 'solemnly admitted that a characteristic of the great saints is their power of "levitation".' With equal solemnity, Chesterton suggests 'they might go further' and admit that another characteristic of the great saints is their 'power of levity'. If levity is indeed a 'power', what kind of power might it be? Another metaphor is used to unlock this one: 'Angels can fly because they can take themselves lightly' (CW 1:325). This throwaway line gives way to an extended digression on how the 'power' of levity is attested in the history, and especially the art history of the Christian tradition. But the line should not be thrown away by the reader, because it says everything and more than may be said by his subsequent references to Fra Angelico and the Pre-Raphaelites. Applying the physical laws of the natural world to the supernatural powers of angels insists more memorably and more perfectly upon the ethical power, the efficacy, of levity, which is the precondition for levitation. 'Angels can fly because they can take themselves lightly' is charming nonsense that makes compelling sense because it does not try to compel us, because it only winks at us through a crack in the semantic

11

meaning created by its pun. The line reminds us that 'light-hearted' must not be equated with frivolity. But it also *shows* us how certain weighty ideas may only be made to fly if they are carried lightly.

Believing that 'nonsense' and 'faith' were 'the two supreme symbolic assertions of the truth that to draw out the soul of things with a syllogism is as impossible as to draw out Leviathan with a hook' (*TD* 49), Chesterton's own methods of enquiry thus forsake the instrumental ambitions of philosophy in favour of what might be called a faith in nonsense. He puts the play of words to serious work, perhaps the most serious work imaginable. Étienne Gilson judged Chesterton's *St Thomas Aquinas* to be 'without possible comparison the best book ever written on St Thomas'. 'Nothing short of genius', Gilson suggests, 'can account for such an achievement'; it proves Chesterton to be 'one of the deepest thinkers who ever existed'. A remarkable verdict coming from such a distinguished philosopher and historian of philosophy. Yet more remarkable is the basis for his praise:

> Everybody will no doubt admit that it is a 'clever' book, but the few readers who have spent twenty or thirty years in studying St. Thomas...cannot fail to perceive that the so-called 'wit' of Chesterton has put their scholarship to shame. He has guessed all that which we had tried to demonstrate, and he has said all that which they were more or less clumsily attempting to express in academic formulas. (*CJ* 510)

What distinguishes Chesterton's 'wit' from his 'so-called wit' is hard to define, especially when purportedly sympathetic readers wield the word like an insult, implying an exclusive allegiance to the aesthetic (where style exists at the expense of substance). It may be that wit is not the most helpful word in the first place. Chesterton provides an alternative. Wit is often used as a loose synonym for humour, but Chesterton makes an instructive distinction between the two. The former, he says, 'is always connected with the idea that truth is close and clear'; the latter, 'with the idea that truth is tricky and mystical and easily mistaken':

> Humour is akin to agnosticism, which is only the negative side of mysticism. But pure wit is akin to Puritanism; to the perfect and

painful consciousness of the final fact in the universe. Very briefly, the man who sees the consistency in things is a wit – and a Calvinist. The man who sees the inconsistency in things is a humorist – and a Catholic. (BS 21)

The occasion for this comment is his study of Bernard Shaw; he is a wit, like Voltaire. When, elsewhere, Chesterton comes to characterize St Francis, wit is never mentioned; it is his sense of humour that is emphasized: it is his humour that 'salts all the stories'; it is his humour that 'prevented him from ever hardening into the solemnity of sectarian self-righteousness' (CW 2:131). Chesterton was certainly capable of wit. But he was generally more generous; warmer, more speculative, and, sometimes, more silly. The difference – to dip into his lexicon once more – is not to be found in the facts of what he wrote but in the 'atmosphere' of his writing.

Basil Grant of The Club of Queer Trades asks 'in a kind of despair': 'are you still so sunk in superstitions, so clinging to dim and prehistoric altars, that you believe in facts?' He explains that, although 'the philosophy of this world may be founded on facts, its business is run on spiritual impressions and atmospheres' (CW 6:88). So too is the business of Chesterton's philosophy run. 'Atmosphere' is the word he uses to paraphrase epochs, people, places, ideas. It is the defining quality in Dickens's fiction that is 'more important than his stories' (CW 15:135); it is the way in which a critic must apply the Aristotelian principles of dramatic unity (not dogmatically, but by attention to their 'artistic atmosphere' (FF 94)); it is what in Mr Barrett's house Robert Browning knew to be 'not a fit thing for any human being, alive, dying, or dead' ('that most poisonous and degrading of all atmospheres – a medical atmosphere') (RB 73;60). The word is worked especially hard when he is wrestling with those matters most elusive but at the same time most important. As when he considers 'the moral atmosphere of the Incarnation' (CW 1:347); or the revelation that comes to Job as 'the terrible and tingling atmosphere of something which is too good to be told' (GC 47).

'Everything', in other words (the words of his mystic poet Gabriel Gale), 'has a sort of atmosphere of what it signifies' (PL 64). And Chesterton does more than describe these atmospheres, he writes about them in an atmospheric way. That does not mean in a vague way. On the contrary, atmosphere means for him something specific and substantial, like 'form', as against 'shape' and 'tint'.[17] The best reconstruction of his thinking is not therefore to be achieved by abstracting his thoughts from their aesthetic contexts, by refining them into some kind of epistemological common currency. We must instead attend closely to 'the very atmosphere of certain words' (CW 16:33); we must consider carefully the way 'every word we use comes to us coloured from all its adventures in history' (WB 1). This kind of close attention is what William Empson meant when he advised that 'it is very necessary for a critic to remember about the atmosphere' of a poem, but that to explain 'atmosphere' the critic 'must concentrate on the whole...rather than on the particular things he can find to say'.[18]

It is a hard thing to write about someone who was always too big for his books. How much harder still if all paraphrase is heresy. He complains that 'All criticism tends too much to become criticism of criticism'; but he also concedes the 'very evident' reason: 'that criticism of creation is so very staggering a thing' (CW 15:177). If one must concentrate on the aesthetic, atmospheric 'whole' rather than on the 'particular things' one can find to say, it is not clear how it is possible to say anything at all. Aesthetic judgement is such a messily-contested business, and Chesterton wrote so much and so variously, that it may seem like the only way to 'create some order out of this mass and variety of material' is by 'the working assumption' that he is 'best studied as a man of ideas'.[19] 'To see Chesterton whole is no easy task': this is readily acknowledged by most critics, but in a way that implies the difficulty is merely one of synthesizing diverse ideas.[20] If the 'problem' of how to 'capture the mind' behind the 'style' without capturing 'the style in which he wrote' is ever raised, it is inevitably only done so in order to dismiss the problem as intractable – before going on to consider his philosophy as if no such problem existed.[21] But even – even, especially – if the expressed intention is to have him 'relaunch the missionary of a Christian intelligentsia in contemporary English society',[22] his intelligence must come fully encumbered of its literariness (which is the opposite of cumbering). What it means to dig for the submerged sunrise of wonder is an aesthetic question before it can be an epistemological one. His thinking cannot be prescinded from his writing because his philosophy must be understood as metaphor before it can be understood as metaphysics. We must attend to the 'atmosphere' of the phrase; we must remember that 'language is not a scientific thing at all, but a wholly artistic thing' (*GW* 91).

Digging is more committed than 'looking', and less cerebral than 'speculating': it is a sweaty praxis. And, what is being dug for is not – as might be expected – something 'buried', it is 'submerged'; and an abstraction of an abstraction ('the sunrise of wonder'). That this pansophic phrase resists translation does not mean that it means nothing. Chesterton elsewhere argues the principle forcibly:

> Much of our modern difficulty, in religion and other things, arises merely from this: that we confuse the word 'indefinable' with the word 'vague.' If someone speaks of a spiritual fact as 'indefinable' we promptly picture something misty, a cloud with indeterminate edges. But this is an error even in commonplace logic. The thing that cannot be defined is the first thing; the primary fact. It is our arms and legs, our pots and pans, that are indefinable. The indefinable is the indisputable... The word that has no definition is the word that has no substitute. If a man falls back again and again on some such word... do not suppose that the word means nothing because he cannot say what it means. If he could say what the word means he would say what it means instead of saying the word... Precisely because the word is indefinable, the word is indispensable. (*CW* 15:39)

If we take 'digging for the submerged sunrise of wonder' to be a defining, indispensible but indefinable expression of Chesterton's philosophy, we are still left with a vexing problem inevitably shirked:[23] what can this hieratic postulate mean? What does it mean to take language aesthetically, metaphorically, in its singular, non-substitutable sense? Hamlet would 'take arms against a sea of troubles'. His sentiment is similarly evanescent, and understanding this line may help to make sense of Chesterton's. The same method is used to opposite outcome. Whereas Hamlet's mixed metaphors expose the vanity of his Canute-like hope (he may take arms against a 'siege' but not against a 'sea'),[24] in Chesterton's phrase, the end is also the means. Taking a shovel to water in search of sunshine is not a self-defeating but a self-describing gesture: innocence is as innocence does. Astonishment awaits us only if we are prepared

15

to treat the world as astonishing. 'It is just as unscientific as it is unphilosophical to be surprised that in an unsympathetic atmosphere certain extraordinary sympathies do not arise' (*CW* 1:357).

Attempting, then, to get at the whole of Chesterton, to read his atmospheres sympathetically – which means poetically as well as philosophically – the following chapters will consider his vastly varied achievements as a writer by genre, in terms of the imaginative gifts that underwrite his work as a whole. The individual chapter headings perhaps threaten to embarrass this hoped-for overview; the contents page promises much but excludes more. Complete coverage is for obvious reasons beyond the scope of this small book. But efforts have been made to consider his minor genres as well. His plays, for instance, receive attention in the chapter on poetry (because some of his drama was in verse), and his literary criticism is considered in the chapter on biography (many of which were literary biographies); and so on. It is for the opposite reason that there is no chapter devoted to his philosophy, or to his theology. These subjects are too *big* to be granted special treatment: 'There is no detail, from buttons to kangaroos, that does not enter in to the gay confusion of philosophy'; 'There is no fact of life, from the death of a donkey to the General Post Office, which has not its place to dance and sing in, in the glorious Carnival of theology' (*GW* 168). Because 'there is nothing that is not relevant' to these subjects, in other words, they are read through all genres of his writing.

There may yet seem something perverse in reading by genre, which emphasizes the diversity of Chesterton's writing, if the aim is to show how everything he wrote is cut from the same scroll. But it is necessary to explore the range of his expression before it is possible to judge the coherence of this thinking. 'To describe adequately his work and him as an author within our usual framework of reference, one would have to make a great many negative statements, such as: his erudition was great, but he was no scholar...he reviewed books and wrote a number of essays on living and dead writers, but he was no literary critic...he thought poetically, but he was neither a poet nor a philosopher'.[25] These comments by Hannah Arendt on Walter Benjamin are applicable to Chesterton too, perhaps even more

16

so. The massif of contrary implications that define his imaginative landscape cannot be mapped in two dimensions. That is why this book evaluates him on his own terms, with a special emphasis on his variousness; and that is also why there is no Conclusion, because the designed independence of the chapters does not submit to the terminal conspectus promised by a linear narrative. Each genre study is, instead, in conversation with each other. It is only by taking mutually correcting bearings that Chesterton can be seen in the round. By extending the interest taken here in certain key words ('innocence' and 'wonder', 'wit' and 'humour', 'queer' and 'paradox', 'facts' and 'atmosphere'; and so on) each chapter aims to refine a working vocabulary, Chesterton's own vocabulary, for the systematic relationship between his diverse writings.

Reading him in his own words does not mean taking him at his word. It means recognizing that neither agreement nor disagreement is possible before it is understood what exactly he meant by what he wrote. Only then (and thereby) can his divided selves, the poet and philosopher, be brought together: to show how, in C. S. Lewis's fine figure, 'The sword glitters not because the swordsman sets out to make it glitter but because he is fighting for his life and therefore moving it very quickly' (CJ 513). This attempt at immanent critique may only be justified in practice. Onwards therefore, encouraged by Chesterton's spirit of recklessly innocent adventure: it is time to take up 'one of those journeys on which a man perpetually feels that now at last he must have come to the end of the universe, and then finds he has only come to the beginning of Tufnell Park' (CW 12:39).

1

Fiction

> Anyhow, I propose on the present occasion to be so perverse as to interest myself in literature when dealing with a literary man; and to be especially interested not only in the literature left by the man but in the philosophy inhering in the literature. (CW 18:49)

Chesterton is today best known as a teller of tales. He would perhaps have been disappointed by this; or at least surprised. 'I have never taken my novels or short stories very seriously, or imagined that I had any particular status in anything so serious as a novel', he reveals in his *Autobiography* (CW 16:313). Without 'vanity or mock modesty', he describes having 'spoilt a number of jolly good ideas' in his fictional works:

> they were not only not as good as a real novelist would have made them, but they were not as good as I might have made them myself, if I had really even been trying to be a real novelist. And among many more abject reasons for not being able to be a novelist, is the fact that I always have been and presumably always shall be a journalist. (CW 16:276)

The reason he could only ever be an accidental writer of fiction is that he preferred seeing 'ideas or notions wrestling naked, as it were, and not dressed up in a masquerade as men and women.' But the reverse suggestion seems more plausible. Given the harlequinade of metaphor and word-play to be found in his non-fiction, his fondness for parable, allegory and anecdotes, and his insouciance when readers uncovered factual errors in his ostensibly factual accounts, it seems more likely that he was unable to be a 'real' journalist because he always was a novelist. The matter is more complicated. He was led by his imagination and relied heavily on his memory. As will be seen in the subsequent chapters, this made him an unconventional writer of non-fiction – but that is not to say an unsuccessful one.

As a writer of fiction, too, he was unconventional; and it is this, not unsuccess, that his disclaimer registers. For he had clear ideas on what he thought the novel was, and should be; and his novels were clearly not of that sort.

Evaluating 'The Great Victorian Novelists', he defines the genre as a narrative told 'for the sake of some study of the difference between human beings' (CW 15:460). That the 'essential' feature of modern fiction is 'the play of personalities in private' is apparently so self-evident that he is content to state rather than argue his position (CW 15:461). 'No clear-headed person wastes his time over definitions,' he explains, 'except where he thinks his own definition would probably be in dispute' (CW 15:460). To dispute his definition is, however, precisely what must be done if his qualities as a writer of fiction are to be appreciated. We may agree that the novel lends itself to a uniquely subtle form of psychological individuation, but disagree that 'a real novelist' may use the genre only in this way. Equally, we may agree that he spoilt a number of jolly good ideas in his fiction, but argue, as a rider, that it was necessary to spoil these ideas for his fiction to work as fiction: because his stories are best when they read least like the ideas that prompted them, and most like the autochthonous ideas of the literature itself. That a novelist need not be realist to be 'real', and that the best 'ideas' in fiction are secured by literary effects, are claims this chapter will show to be directly related.

E. M. Forster's attempt to distinguish between 'flat' and 'round' characters stumbles when it comes to Dickens. Forster cites Dickens as a paradigm author of 'what were called "humours" in the seventeenth century, and are sometimes called types, and sometimes caricatures'. 'In their purest form', flat characters 'are constructed round a single idea or quality': 'The really flat characters can be expressed in one sentence such as "I never will desert Mr Micawber"'.[1] Forster has no sooner begun down this road than he finds himself in difficulty. Although 'Dickens's people are nearly all flat', 'flat' proves too flat a term to describe how these people behave: 'Nearly everyone can be summed up in a sentence, and yet there is this wonderful feeling of human depth.' What explains this wonderful feeling? Forster has no idea. He can only manage a sentence of speculation whose vagueness is confessed in its first word: 'Probably the immense vitality of Dickens causes his characters to vibrate a little, so that they borrow his life and appear to lead one of their own.' Forster goes on to say that those who dislike Dickens have 'an excellent case', because he 'ought to be bad'. And yet: 'He is actually one of our big writers, and his immense success with types suggests that there may be more in flatness than the severer critics admit'.[2]

This is a refreshingly honest hands-ups from the critic; a triumph of intuition over his own schematic thinking. It was not, however, an original intuition. Chesterton had already argued the same in *The Victorian Age in Literature* (1913), which was reprinted eight times before Forster delivered his Clark lectures (in which his 'flat' versus 'round' characters thesis was first presented (1927)). Moreover, Chesterton is able to do what Forster cannot. He can see that Dickens's characters are 'at once so plainly creations and so plainly caricatures' (*CW* 16:313). But he can also explain what nonetheless causes the wonderful feeling of human depth:

> The art of Dickens was that most exquisite of arts: it was the art of enjoying everybody...I do not for a moment maintain that he enjoyed everybody in his everyday life. But he enjoyed everybody in his books; and everybody has enjoyed everybody in those books even till to-day. His books are full of baffled villains stalking out or cowardly bullies kicked downstairs. But the villains and the cowards are such delightful people that the reader always hopes the villain will put his head through a side window and make a last remark; or that the bully will say one thing more, even from the bottom of the stairs. The reader hopes this; and he cannot get rid of the fancy that the author hopes so too. (*CW* 15:472–3)

Flat characters are, Forster observes, often 'best when they are comic';[3] and this is important to remember. But Chesterton understood something more important: that Dickens's infectious enjoyment of his characters is not only comic, it is also ethical:

> ... he had broad or universal sympathies in a sense totally unknown to the social reformers who wallow in such phrases. Dickens (unlike the social reformers) really did sympathize with every sort of victim of every sort of tyrant...Dickens did not merely believe in the brotherhood of men in the weak modern way; he was the brotherhood of men, and knew it was a brotherhood in sin as well as in aspiration. (*CW* 15:473–4)

Turning Chesterton's critique back onto his own fiction here reveals a palmary affinity between these writers in the way they prevent their characters from becoming ciphers, and their stories from being over-determined by the ideas that inspired them. Such dogma as there is in Chesterton's fiction takes the form of a refusal of ideas, and social structures, that affront his 'universal sympathies'. This is never seen more clearly than in his most famous fictional creation. Father Brown is a priest who is also an amateur detective. Both his vocation and his hobby might be thought to demand a polarized view, of evil versus good, and law versus lawlessness. But the dozens of short stories in which Father Brown stars encourage the opposite. We first meet the 'little Norfolk priest' on the hunt for a master criminal by the name of Flambeau, where we are teased with a promise:

> It is many years now since this colossus of crime suddenly ceased keeping the world in turmoil; and when he ceased, as they said after the death of Roland, there was a great quiet upon the earth. But in his best days (I mean, of course, his worst) Flambeau was a figure as statuesque and international as the Kaiser. (CW 12:31)

The tease is in the tense. Even as the story suspensefully unfolds, the narrative retrospect assures that Flambeau's criminal career will come to an end (we are also told that the head of the Paris police was primed to make 'the greatest arrest of the century' (CW 12:31)). But his career does not end here. When it eventually does, three stories later, it is not, as might be expected, with his death. Unlike the Frankish military governor of the Breton March with whom he is here compared, Flambeau is not killed. Nor is he captured. What Chesterton found lamentably lacking in contemporary 'serious fiction' was that it failed to go anywhere, that it failed to end, 'not only in the modern sense of an ending, but in the medieval sense of a fruition' (AG 83). His own stories, by contrast, possess what he called philosophical 'purpose'; their endings ('in the modern sense') express themselves in the medieval sense of an ending as something more like a beginning. Flambeau is not criminalized, he is converted.

By the fifth story, Father Brown is introduced by Flambeau as 'my friend'; and Flambeau features thereafter in many of the

21

subsequent adventures as poacher turned game keeper. The tease, then, is not a reassurance, it is an unsettling: an inversion of our expectations for what reassurance might mean. The man of God and the law does not arrest the wicked man by taking away his liberty; he arrests his wickedness by liberating him into the possibility that he could be good. This inversion, this redemption, is sustained by Chesterton thoroughly 'enjoying' Flambeau. The parenthetical clarification of the passage quoted above reveals this implicitly. We are invited to admire just how good he is at being bad. The appreciative adjectives of this passage ('colossus', 'statuesque') are matched with others commending his 'gigantic stature and bodily daring', his 'fantastic physical strength' and his 'startling' acrobatics (*CW* 12:31–2).

It is, however, the mind behind the crimes – specifically, the aesthetic touches of his ill-doing – that wins most approval. Such as when 'he once repainted all the numbers in a street in the dead of night merely to divert one traveller into a trap' (*CW* 12:32). Or, in another story, when he lures a policeman 'into the queerest trap ever set in the world': 'on to the stage of a Christmas pantomime, where he could be kicked, clubbed, stunned and drugged' by Flambeau playing the impeccant part of a dancing harlequin, 'amid roars of laughter from all the most respectable people in Putney' (*CW* 12:101). Even after his redemption, 'in his highly moral old age', Flambeau holds that his crimes had been 'beautiful':

> As an artist I had always attempted to provide crimes suitable to the special season or landscapes in which I found myself, choosing this or that terrace or garden for a catastrophe, as if for a statuary group. Thus squires should be swindled in long rooms panelled with oak; while Jews, on the other hand, should rather find themselves unexpectedly penniless among the lights and screens of the Café Riche. Thus, in England, if I wished to relieve a dean of his riches (which is not so easy as you might suppose), I wished to frame him, if I make myself clear, in the green lawns and grey towers of some cathedral town. Similarly, in France, when I had got money out of a rich and wicked peasant (which is almost impossible), it gratified me to get his indignant head relieved against a grey line of clipped poplars, and those solemn plains of Gaul over which broods the mighty spirit of Millet. (*CW* 12:89)

The integrity of Flambeau's delinquency is endorsed by Father Brown, who calls him a 'genius', a 'poet' and an 'honest outlaw' (CW 12:101). What is implied by Brown's sympathy is not immediately clear. Sherlock Holmes concedes the cunning of his arch-nemesis, whom he describes as having 'extraordinary mental powers' (especially in respect of his 'phenomenal mathematical faculty'). But there is an important difference. Although Professor Moriarty is a worthy adversary – sharing the same 'high, domed forehead' that marks Holmes's prodigious intellect – he is identified also as having 'hereditary tendencies of the most diabolical kind.'[4] His badness is therefore as inevitable as his greatness; they are set at birth. And so, when Holmes and Moriarty meet in 'The Final Problem', when they are locked in mortal combat atop the Reichenbach Falls, there is never any chance that the 'problem' will prove 'final' other than in death. How different this is to the first time Father Brown meets Flambeau, when they too are locked in physical struggle. The event is told by Father Brown, who unexpectedly emerges with the 'celebrated set of fish knives and forks' of the exclusive club of The Twelve True Fisherman that had been stolen just moments before. "I don't know his real name", said the priest placidly; "but I know something of his fighting weight, and a great deal about his spiritual difficulties. I formed the physical estimate when he was trying to throttle me, and the moral estimate when he repented"' (CW 12:83).

In Browning's dramatic monologues, Chesterton finds 'a kind of cosmic detective who walked into the foulest of thieves' kitchens and accused men publicly of virtue'; 'Charity was his basic philosophy; but it was, as it were, a fierce charity, a charity that went man-hunting' (RB 52). The Father Brown stories almost read like a designed example of the same. Wilfully misunderstanding the question as to whether he managed to catch Flambeau, Father Brown replies, 'I caught him, with an unseen hook and an invisible line which is long enough to let him wander to the ends of the world, and still to bring him back with a twitch upon the thread' (CW 12:84). This ironical patter is in danger of sounding smug. But the story as it unfolds is more modest and appealing than that, and so is Father Brown. It takes several further pages to explain how Flambeau had stolen the silverware, and how Father Brown discovered him. These revelations provide the satisfying detective-tale denouement. They also provide an ethical context for Flambeau's behaviour, and Father Brown's as well.

Here is the moment where one of the genuine waiters realizes a crime has been committed. By stopping in his tracks, he excites a 'strange shame' in the gentlemen he is meant to be serving that is described as 'wholly the product of our time':

> It is the combination of modern humanitarianism with the horrible modern abyss between the souls of the rich and poor. A genuine historic aristocrat would have thrown things at the waiter, beginning with empty bottles, and very probably ending with money. A genuine democrat would have asked him, with comrade-like clearness of speech, what the devil he was doing. But these modern plutocrats could not bear a poor man near to them, either as a slave or as a friend. That something had gone wrong with the servants was merely a dull, hot embarrassment. They did not want to be brutal, and they dreaded the need to be benevolent. They wanted the thing, whatever it was, to be over. It was over. The waiter, after standing for some seconds rigid, like a cataleptic, turned round and ran madly out of the room. (CW 12:80)

It is precisely this 'horrible modern abyss between the souls of the rich and poor' that makes the theft possible in the first place. Flambeau exploits 'the plain fact that a gentleman's evening dress is the same as a waiter's'. But the explanation cannot after all be so plain. He is able to pass undetected among the gentlemen by moving 'in the lightning style of a waiter, with bent head, flapping napkin and flying feet', just as he is among the waiters, by assuming 'the absent-minded insolence which they have all seen in their patrons' (CW 12:86). The symmetry of his crime ostends an elaborate social idiocy – a moral crime – in which both parties are complicit. The 'abyss' yawns so wide that, even with everyone dressed identically, men cannot see how the common humanity between rich and poor makes these categories reversible.

Father Brown approves of the crime aesthetically, for its simplicity (comparing it to *Hamlet*, no less, he proposes that 'every work of art, divine or diabolic' has the same 'indispensable mark', 'that the centre of it is simple' (CW 12:85–6)). Less obviously, though more significantly, there is also a sense in which he approves of the crime in ethical terms. Chesterton elsewhere writes of how he once escaped being arrested by two policemen who caught him 'throwing a big Swedish knife at a tree, practising (alas, without success) that useful trick of knife-throwing by which men murder each other in Stevenson's romances'. He explains his harmless fun, and is believed. But no sooner has he persuaded the policemen of his intentions than he demands to be taken into custody – because he reads the 'peculiar philosophical importance' of the incident. That the policemen take his word, when he has nothing but his word to offer, exposes 'a great national sin', 'our great English vice; to be watched more fiercely than small-pox': 'the habit of respecting a gentleman'.[5]

Father Brown first became suspicious when he heard two different kinds of tread made by the same feet pass his door in rotation: 'doing a dance that was as queer as the dance of death'. He identifies the first as 'the walk of a well-fed gentleman waiting for something, who strolls about rather because he is physically alert than because he is impatient'. He cannot place the second, until he hears the clink of some plates. Whereupon: 'I saw the nature of the crime, as clearly as if I were going to commit it' (CW 12:85). This is no idle figure of speech. In a preamble to the fourth collection of stories, Father Brown reluctantly tells the 'secret' of his method. It involves something more than trying to 'reconstruct the psychology' of the criminal class:

> I mean that I really did see myself, and my real self, committing the murders. I didn't actually kill the men by material means; but that's not the point. Any brick or bit of machinery might have killed them by material means. I mean that I thought and thought about how a man might come to be like that, until I realized that I really *was* like that, in everything except actual final consent to action. (CW 13:218)

This exercise is not 'scientific'; it is 'religious', because it does not treat the crime and the criminal from the outside but from the inside. To approach detection and criminology as a science means studying man 'in what they call a dry impartial light, in what I would call a dead and dehumanized light':

> They mean getting a long way off him, as if he were a distant prehistoric monster; staring at the shape of his 'criminal skull' as if it were a sort of eerie growth, like the horn on a rhinoceros's nose.

When the scientist talks about a type, he never means himself, but always his neighbour; probably his poorer neighbour. I don't deny the dry light may sometimes do good; though in one sense it's the very reverse of science. So far from being knowledge, it's actually suppression of what we know. It's treating a friend as a stranger, and pretending that something familiar is really remote and mysterious. (*CW* 13:218–9)

Father Brown's treatment of the criminal as a human being, and the stranger as a friend with whom he shares an essential commonality, recalls the charitable impulse of William Cobbett, whose 'sense of human equality' was that he could 'sympathise from the *inside*' (*WC* 215; emphasis mine). For Chesterton, though, the paragon of this radical empathy is St Francis of Assisi. To describe him as 'very nearly the opposite of a philanthropist' seems like a surprising aspersion for Chesterton to cast; but it is no *bêtise* or blasphemy. He wishes to expose a pedantry in the Greek word that carries something like a satire on itself (meaning 'one who loves anthropoids'); and thereby, to press a philological into a philosophical distinction: that 'St. Francis did not love humanity but men' (*CW* 2:29–30). The 'extraordinary personal power' of that 'very genuine democrat' who was oblivious to status – 'from the Pope to the beggar, from the sultan of Syria in his pavilion to the ragged robbers crawling out of the wood' – arose, Chesterton suggests, from his being 'really interested' in every man's '*inner* individual life' (*CW* 2:88–9; emphasis mine). Robert Browning 'was not content with seeking sinners – he sought the sinners whom even sinners cast out' (*RB* 52). St Francis went further still: he inspired 'the first whisper of that wild blessing that afterwards took the form of a blasphemy: "He listens to those to whom God himself will not listen"' (*CW* 2:52). If it was, then, the literary creations of Dickens and Browning (and to some extent Walter Scott)[6] who showed Chesterton that villains could be loveable types, it was the life example of St Francis (and to some extent Cobbett) who taught him they could be capable of love.

Jorge Luis Borges contends that the Father Brown stories 'are the key to Chesterton, the symbols and reflections of Chesterton'; 'an abbreviation' of his life.[7] It is tempting to agree. Except that Borges interprets this 'key', these 'symbols and reflections', not in terms of the extension of Dickensian brotherhood, but as an extension of Dickensian Gothicism. Borges does not find in these stories Chesterton's emulation of the universal sympathy he lauded in the life of St Francis, but a sublimation of the nightmarish atrocities he admired in *Grimm's Fairy Tales*. Surprisingly, these positions are compatible, even mutually illuminating. The reason is to be found in his own criticism on Dickens, that: 'In order of artistic value, next after his humour comes his horror. And both his humour and his horror are of a kind strictly to be called human; that is, they belong to the basic part of us, below the lowest roots of our variety' (*CW* 15:100). Or, as he elsewhere writes by way of introducing some 'trivial fragments' of his non-fiction:

> This row of shapeless and ungainly monsters which I now set before the reader does not consist of separate idols cut out capriciously in lonely valleys or various islands. These monsters are meant for the gargoyles of a definite cathedral. I have to carve the gargoyles, because I can carve nothing else; I leave to others the angels and the arches and the spires. But I am very sure of the style of the architecture, and of the consecration of the church. (*AD* 7)

Reading the reference to gargoyles and cathedrals within the wider context of Chesterton's thoughts on 'the meaning of the grotesque' and 'the three great stages of art', it is clear that his Gothic temperament is not opposed to his Christian convictions, but to Apollonian classicism.[8] Most of all, he is opposed – his Gothicism is the opposite of – the modern style and sensibility known as Realism. For Realism presents life faithfully in all its grotesquerie. Gothicism, he believed, presents the same advance of Shakespeare upon Sophocles but with the difference that its 'atmosphere' is a nightmare that may startle us into noticing a redeeming underlying order of which nightmarishness is the negation. Although Chesterton seems to take a lugubrious relish in creating nothing but gargoyles, that is not inconsistent with sympathy for the angels. A closer look at the way he incubates the incubi of his fiction provides a context for his comment that 'one branch of the beautiful is the ugly', and that there is a 'legitimate liberty' in the 'grotesque' (*CW* 2:234).

When it was published, *The Man Who Was Thursday* attracted much amused attention. Referring to his supposed 'festive views', some readers affected to mistake it for *The Man Who Was Thirsty*. Others, 'naturally supposed' that Man Thursday was 'the black brother of Man Friday'. Perhaps the majority then and now treated it 'as a mere title out of topsyturvydom'; that is, as nonsense (*CW* 16:103). It exasperated Chesterton less that people misread his title than that 'hardly anybody' read the subtitle. That the book is framed as 'A Nightmare' is, he advised, 'the answer to a good many critical questions' (*CW* 16:103). But what kind of answer is it?

He explains: 'the point is that the whole story is a nightmare of things, not as they are, but as they seemed to the young half-pessimist of the '90s... So far as the story had any sense in it, it was meant to begin with the picture of the world at its worst and to work towards the suggestion that the picture was not so black' (*CW* 16:103–4). For its phantasmagoria, then, the tale resists easy analogizing. That did not stop contemporary readers interpreting the book as Christian allegory, and the character of 'Sunday' as Christ. And it has not stopped modern readers doing the same. Biblical echoes give credence to the idea that the 'identification of Sunday as God – and in a very particular way as God incarnate – is confirmed in the text of the novel'.[9] Such a conclusion cannot be satisfying, however. The impulse to read Chaucer's Canterbury pilgrims as ciphers is met by Chesterton with a sardonically modest proposal, apposite here. 'But I have myself a dark suspicion that Chaucer was writing a poem, and especially telling a story; and that to him as an artist the vivid and coloured figures of [for instance] the Summoner and the Friar were of much more importance than the interests they represented in ecclesiastical law' (*CW* 18:186).

More specifically, reading *The Man Who Was Thursday* as Christian allegory refuses Chesterton's subtitle, and the explanation of his subtitle (that Sunday 'the pantomime ogre' cannot stand even as 'a blasphemous version of the Creator'). The allegorical urge refuses also the 'atmosphere' of the novel that makes sense of its subtitle: because everything about the novel is dreamlike, and much of this oneiric mood has a nightmarish tinge. The gorgeous pathetic fallacy of the story's opening describes Saffron Park, a suburb 'on the sunset side of London' with an evening's sky that 'looked like the end of the world'; it is a place the visitor would find 'not only pleasant, but perfect, if once he could regard it not as a deception but rather as a dream' (*CW* 6:475). Like the visitor, the reader entering this new world is snagged on that conditional 'if'. From the very first clash between the two poets who argue over 'the whole nature of poetry', the easy dreaminess of the narrative is troubled by a thoroughly pervasive sense of deception. When Gabriel Syme declares himself 'a poet of law, a poet of order', and Gregory identifies the artist as 'identical with an anarchist', they both wilfully mislead (as, in *The Club of Queer Trades*, Lieutenant Drummond Keith unwittingly misleads) by being so completely literal in their veracity. The subsequent revelation that, as well as being a poet, Syme is a policeman, and Gregory an anarchist, is emblematic of the sheer instability – which is also the stable philosophy – of this created world: being so completely upset in its right order that everything is taken for its opposite, the best way to disguise the truth is to confess it.

So it is that the secret anarchists' Council positively 'flaunt' themselves by freely discussing their intentions on a balcony overlooking Leicester Square. By inviting suspicion, they may best avoid it: being taken for a lot of jolly gentlemen too open to have secrets, too playful to be serious, their wickedness may be taken for whimsy. But, of course, we later learn that even that double-bluff is doubled. Syme's outrageous ruse by which he manages to get elected onto the Council by denouncing Gregory for being insufficiently committed to anarchism is an irony that ripens and recoils, as subsequent chapters reveal that everyone on the Council is actually an undercover policeman pretending to be an anarchist in order to catch anarchists.

A highlight of these anarchists' unmaskings is that of the lame and myopic Professor de Worms. No sooner is the reader steadied by the explanation that the Professor managed to pursue Syme with such startling speed, agility and stamina half way across London because he is in fact a fit young actor by the name of Wilks; no sooner this return to reasonableness than the story is given another vertiginous spin, with the explanation of how Wilks came to assume the persona of the Professor in the first place. The disguise was, it turns out, not originally intended as a mask but as a mirror. Wilks had intended to make a parodic protest against the 'the great German Nihilist philosopher, Professor de Worms', until, unexpectedly, he found that it was his caricature who was taken for the authentic Professor, and it was the real Professor who was thought 'a preposterous parody'.

(The real Professor is now received everywhere in Europe as a delightful impostor, 'his apparent earnestness and anger' making him 'all the more entertaining'.) Wilks explains that he was credible as the Professor not because he was anything like him, but because he was so unlike him. Being an old man in poor health, the Professor 'could not be expected to be so impressively feeble as a young actor in the prime of life'. The same strategy of excess and inversion was used to secure his academic credentials too. Whenever the real Professor said something that nobody but he could understand, Wilks replied with something he could not even understand himself:

> 'I don't fancy,' he said, 'that you could have worked out the principle that evolution is only negation, since there inheres in it the introduction of lacuna, which are an essential of differentiation.' I replied quite scornfully, 'You read all that up in Pinckwerts; the notion that involution functioned eugenically was exposed long ago by Glumpe.' It is unnecessary for me to say that there never were such people as Pinckwerts and Glumpe. But the people all round (rather to my surprise) seemed to remember them quite well, and the Professor, finding that the learned and mysterious method left him rather at the mercy of an enemy slightly deficient in scruples, fell back upon a more popular form of wit. 'I see,' he sneered, 'you prevail like the false pig in Aesop.' 'And you fail,' I answered, smiling, 'like the hedgehog in Montaigne.' Need I say that there is no hedgehog in Montaigne? (CW 6:550–51)

With each chapter further layers of reality are stripped away to reveal unreality, and surreality. Finally, we learn that even the feared leader of the Council, 'Sunday', turns out to be a policeman (or at least someone who posed as a policeman), for he was the man in the dark room who first recruited all the other policemen of the Council. What emerges from these shifting shapes is presented as a kind of knowledge that is a warrant. In the final chapter, 'The Accuser', Lucien Gregory returns to confront Syme. He convicts him and the other spurious anarchists (and the police and the government they support) of 'the unpardonable sin' of 'supreme power', 'that it is supreme':

> 'I do not curse you for being cruel. I do not curse you (though I might) for being kind. I curse you for being safe! You sit in your chairs of stone, and have never come down from them. You are the

seven angels of heaven, and you have had no troubles. Oh, I could forgive you everything, you that rule all mankind, if I could feel for once that you had suffered for one hour a real agony such as I –' (*CW* 6:633)

Syme repels the slander. He and the rest of the Council have, he says, been 'broken' by their experiences. Not only have they descended from their thrones, they have 'descended into hell'. Their experiences have taught them 'that each man fighting for order may be as brave and good a man as the dynamiter'. They have, in short, earned the right to answer the accuser, 'We also have suffered' (*CW* 6:634).

It is worth pausing over these words. A. N. Wilson has described Chesterton as 'a thinker with no sense of darkness'; his apparent failure 'to grasp the widely held conviction that Christianity, with the cross at its centre, presents a sombre picture of the world, albeit one in which tragedy is ultimately eclipsed by hope' is, Wilson suggests, 'a huge and damaging gap' in his theology. Wilson goes on to cite Dietrich Bonhoeffer's view that he could only worship a God who had suffered.[10] But the first lesson to learn in reading Chesterton is that his play with language is serious stuff: his conviction that 'The cross is the crux of the whole matter' (*CW* 2:266) is a pun that may be earnest without being 'sombre'. The second, related lesson to learn is that Chesterton's 'sense of darkness' is often to be found in his lightest fiction. Precisely the burden of this book is to show that Chesterton cannot be understood until he is read in this way, in the round: his literature read philosophically, and his philosophy for the way it expresses itself by a form of literary thinking. If *Orthodoxy* posits but does not explore 'positive evil' in the world (*CW* 1:217), the real presence of evil is the dark preoccupation of his drawing-room drama, *Magic*; if suffering seems curiously absent in *Orthodoxy*, it is curiously present in the knock-about dottiness of *The Man Who Was Thursday*, in this climactic scene just described. And so on.

It is not that Chesterton can only imagine darkness when safely packaged in the imaginary. His theology is directly defined against the darkness of which he had personal experience: a whole chapter in his *Autobiography* is devoted to describing 'knowing the devil' in the 'doubts and morbidities and temptations' of his youth (*CW* 16:85). The subtitle of *The*

Man Who Was Thursday announces a nightmare, but it is one he had really lived through: the epigraph verses to the novel describe his witness of 'old fears' and 'emptied hells' that he only now 'may safely write'. If his theological writing emphasizes the sheer joy of his faith, he finds a balance in the theology of his writing that does not announce itself as theological. Bonhoeffer's warrant of empathy – the authority to answer the accuser, 'We also have suffered' – is also at the heart of Father Brown's ambition to inhabit the mind of the criminal:

> No man's really any good till he knows how bad he is, or might be; till he's realized exactly how much right he has to all this snobbery, and sneering, and talking about 'criminals,' as if they were apes in a forest ten thousand miles away; till he's got rid of all the dirty self-deception of talking about low types and deficient skulls; till he's squeezed out of his soul the last drop of the oil of the Pharisees; till his only hope is somehow or other to have captured one criminal, and kept him safe and sane under his own hat. (*CW* 13:219)

Syme and the members of the Council have learnt how bad they can be, by becoming the bad men they are trying to catch: and they have seen that they are men like themselves – so like themselves indeed that the policemen prove indistinguishable from the anarchists. Just as – from the opposite point of view, but by the same principle – waiters and gentlemen are always distinguishable, even though they wear the same clothes, and may even be the same person wearing the same clothes. Chesterton's stories seem consistently to affirm the unique authority of that deity who 'from all the gods in the world' is the only one who became a man, and was tempted: the only one 'who has himself been in revolt', 'who ever suffered their isolation', who, even, 'seemed for an instant to be an atheist' (*CW* 1:343).

But, not so fast. Chesterton cannot be read as if he merely decanted his faith into his fiction. There is a danger of over-determining the ethics of his fiction by conflating it with his faith, and this danger is not restricted to those who would have Chesterton speak for radical orthodoxy.[11] The problem with reading his stories as if they were the authentic expression of his religion denies, for start, that his fiction may be just that, a fiction. Reading all genres of his work as if they were a paraphrase of the same (Christian) thought denies also the possibility that the respective chapters of this book aim to demonstrate: that different kinds of writing may express different things, things that are untranslatable without remainder from one genre into another.

A third problem in equating his fiction with the precepts of his faith is that it denies Chesterton the opportunity of thinking anything outside Roman rule. It may be that the Lord's prayer 'makes clear in its very first phrase' that it 'postulates the brotherhood of all men',[12] and that the same postulate is at the imaginative innermost of Chesterton's fiction. But this is true of his writing decades before his conversion, and may be felt throughout his fiction without the necessary feeling that it is catholic because he is Catholic; it is the other way around.

Consider one final expression of this universal brotherhood. Chesterton was much interested in madness, partly for personal reasons. His *Autobiography* describes in detail the 'lunatic' period in his youth, and he explores related questions on the causes and correct estimation of insanity in a great many of his stories. R. D. Laing would scandalize the psychiatric schools of the late twentieth century by treating the content of psychotic behavior as a valid expression of distress – because, under certain conditions, madness may be the sanest response to late modernity. Chesterton anticipates this polemic. Except that the apparent lunacy of his characters tends to be expressed through joy; their symptoms are less like madness than madcappery. 'Alone among the animals', Chesterton suggests, man is 'shaken with the beautiful madness called laughter; as if he caught sight of some secret in the very shape of the universe hidden from the universe itself' (CW 2:168). The possibility of such a secret, or at least the beauty of such laughter, steers him away from melancholia. But his lunatics are no less philosophically significant for that.

The Ball and the Cross explores the idea that 'the modern world is organized in relation to the most obvious and urgent of all questions, not so much to answer it wrongly, as to prevent it being answered at all' (CW 16:288). The novel's protagonists, Turnbull and MacIan, jump over a wall to evade the police, only to find they have inadvertently broken into a mental asylum from which the doctors will not let them leave. This unexpected destination has more sinister implications than their yachting misadventure to the Isle of Thanet (noted in the *Introduction*). Because it turns out that the ambition of the police who are chasing the duelists is shared by the devil. Their arrival and detention, we learn, was not accidental at all, it was planned by the one with eyes that 'seemed to be made of ironies behind ironies, as two mirrors infinitely reflect each other' (*CW* 7:215).

More broadly, the treatment of lunacy in this book, and in many other stories (notably, *The Poet and the Lunatics*, *The Man Who Knew Too Much* and *Manalive*) is a deceptively jocose insistence on the same democratic morality identified above.[13] It is an insistence that the categories by which society raises some men up and keep others down are arbitrary, precarious and, at root, unethical. By dramatizing the ways in which these categories divide men from one another (whether by class, criminality or mental health), he makes a countervailing appeal of universal sympathy. And this appeal is appealing precisely because it is aesthetic and not didactic, because of the non-fungible ways that it is dramatic, suspenseful, funny.

Chesterton writes of a 'quality running through all' the teaching of Christ, something 'neglected in most modern talk about them as teachings': 'the persistent suggestion' that Christ 'has not really come to teach'. Illustrating his point, he recalls the miracle of the wines at Canaan which affects him 'personally' for being 'grandly and gloriously human... in the sense in which a whole crowd of prigs, having the appearance of human beings, can hardly be described as human'. It is 'grandly and gloriously human' because it is celebratory, because it is about men revelling in life and love: because it is 'as democratic as Dickens' (*CW* 2:337). The miracle, he says, strikes 'a note of things not fully explained' (*CW* 2:337). So too does Chesterton's fiction strike us. What we sense is not the intrusion of a doctrine, but a pungent 'atmosphere'.

Reflecting on 'the groping and guesswork philosophy' that informed the composition of *The Man Who Was Thursday*, he waves away the idea that the book might prove he was a 'Pantheist', or a 'Pagan'; or that its denouement 'was an interpolation by priests'. He quotes instead a tribute from 'a distinguished psycho-analyst, of the most modern and scientific sort', who had found *The Man Who Was Thursday* to be 'useful as

a corrective among his morbid patients; especially the process
by which each of the diabolical anarchs turns out to be a good
citizen in disguise. '"I know a number of men who nearly went
mad", he said quite gravely, "but were saved because they really
understood *The Man Who Was Thursday*"' (*CW* 16:104–5).
   Because they 'really understood' what? Because they really
understood the book's atmosphere. Just as Chesterton believed
an 'inconvenience' to be 'only an adventure wrongly considered' (*AC* 36), the 'nightmare' announced in the subtitle of *The
Man Who Was Thursday* is revealed to be only a dream wrongly
considered (the anarchs are policemen). This is the defining
atmosphere of Chesterton's fiction. The 'misunderstanding' of
the mystery story 'is only meant as a dark outline of a cloud to
bring out the brightness of that instant intelligibility';[14] it is the
gargoyles who announce the Gothic Church: 'it is the supreme
function of the philosopher of the grotesque to make the world
stand on its head that people may look at it' (*RB* 151). That
madness might be alleviated by understanding; that the world is
better than pessimists presume: this conviction recurs with a
particular Catholic vocabulary after his conversion, but the idea
is already present and puissant before this time. Even during his
youthful years of self-described 'lunacy', he fervently held that:
'Even if the very daylight were a dream, it was a day-dream; it
was not a nightmare'. 'Anything', he felt, 'was magnificent as
compared with nothing' (*CW* 16:96). For all the darkness of
Chesterton's tales – in many ways because of their darkness – it
is the magnificence of existence that shines through.

2

Poetry

> The critics were wrong in the worst way in which a critic can be wrong about a poem: in being wrong about the point of it. (*AG* 208)

To get at what kind of poet Chesterton was it is helpful, first, to be clear about what kind he was not. Ezra Pound's poetic imagination, for instance, is scaled to the concrete image, and G. M. Hopkins's to the abruptly stressed phrase; Christopher Marlowe is known for his mighty line, and Alexander Pope for the *soigné* couplet. Chesterton wrote galloping stanzas. This makes him different from each of these poets individually, but it also makes him different from them as a group. The reason he writes at the tempo and according to the prosodic proportions he does is that he is not actually a poet at all. Those who are the first to agree on this – those who think him too careless, too fey, or too political – are generally the last to recognize that he was not, either, trying to be one. They make the category error of presuming that if he is not a good poet he must be a failed poet. But what he aimed to be, and what he is, is something deliberately different.

Chesterton's poetical imagination expresses itself as it does because he is a balladeer. By dilating his meaning across several lines he is able to reduce the 'intensity of interpretation upon the grammar' that Empson describes as the inevitable result of writing in metre.[1] For what is lost in expressive 'ambiguity' there is a corresponding gain in clarity. This is important because, for the ballad, what is required above all is that the narrative may be understood at first reading (or hearing). In Chesterton's case, what is required is that the narrative may be understood even at *fast* reading, because it is through an accelerated prosody – together with suspended syntax, anapho-

36

ric repetitions, abrupt alliteration and clinching end rhymes – that his verses generate their defining 'atmosphere', which is dramatic.

In other words, Chesterton did not write poetry, he wrote verse, the relative merit of which cannot be determined by criteria used to appraise poetry. It is truer to say that the criteria must be inverted. We wince at his rousing and rollicking only if we expect to find the kinds of parataxis, abstraction and equivocal allusion that characterize the dominant poetic culture of his peers. We are embarrassed and unmoved by his martellato rhythms only if we are hoping for less emphatic, and more eccentric cadences. T. S. Eliot declared 'that poets in our civilization, as it exists at present must be *difficult*',[2] and Chesterton's poetry is determinedly not that. But, to do him justice, Eliot was also aware that there is 'a type of verse for the appreciation of which we are not provided with the proper critical tools'. Eliot is thinking here about the 'modern ballad'. The context for his comment is an apology for Rudyard Kipling, and what he says of Kipling's verse may be directly applied to Chesterton's too (Eliot implicitly makes the connexion between Kipling and Chesterton himself, in his qualified commendation of Chesterton's verse as 'first-rate journalistic balladry' (*CJ* 531)). Whereas most modern poets must be defended 'against the charge of obscurity', or of writing poems that do 'not appear to scan', Chesterton must be defended 'against the charge of excessive lucidity', and 'of writing jingles'.[3]

The 'proper' critical tools with which to appreciate Chesterton must, then, be sensitive to the cumulative drama of his verses rather than to their localized moments of interest: they must register how his stanzas are so forcible. He shakes his head at Bernard Shaw for not inspiring 'the three forms of human utterance which come next in nobility to a prayer': 'the war-song', 'the drinking-song' and 'the love-song' (*BS* 101). When it came to verse, Chesterton wrote little else. Although he works within remarkably various prosodic forms, always, their virtues lie in the directness of their appeal. However far he strayed from the prototypical ballad stanza (abcb quatrains of iambic tetrameter, or trimiter), he remains faithful to the plangency of the ballad tradition that beats its drum, and occasionally thumps its tub, against the *mauvaise honte* reluctance of modernity.

That is not to say he never produces richly subtle moments, it is to say that these moments are expressed through the simplicity of his verses. There is a curious sense in which his achievement as a poet is in excess of his purpose as a versifier; a sort of accidental over-spilling of his analogical imagination that is at the same time a considered strategy from one who believed that 'the innermost part of all poetry is the nursery rhyme' (*FF* 2). For this reason, his verse is best appreciated when one does not look for poetry in it. Because then, as Eliot said of Kipling: 'the poetry, when it comes, owes the gravity of its impact to being something over and above the bargain, something more than the writer undertook to give you; and that the matter is never simply a pretext, an occasion for poetry'.[4] The extent to which Chesterton was conscious of this over-spilling is suggested in his essay on 'The Romance of Rhyme'. Taking rhyme as a metonym for verse, he argues that the 'whole history of the thing...can be found between these two things: the simple pleasure of rhyming "diddle" to "fiddle", and the more sophisticated pleasure of rhyming "diddle"to "idyll"' (*FF* 2):

> Now the fatal mistake about poetry, and more than half the fatal mistake about humanity, consists in forgetting that we should have the first kind of pleasure as well as the second. It might be said we should have the first type of pleasure as the basis of the second; or yet more truly, the first pleasure inside the second.

It is time to examine the simple and sophisticated pleasures of Chesterton's verse close-up. 'The Ballad of the White Horse' is an idealized tale of the Saxon King Alfred the Great, and in it Chesterton shows how well he can make his stanzas roar. Here is the first charge:

> Roaring they went o'er the Roman wall,
>   And roaring up the lane,
> Their torches tossed, a ladder of fire,
> Higher their hymn was heard and higher,
> More sweet for hate and for heart's desire,
> And up in the northern scrub and brier,
>   They fell upon the Dane.

(*CP* 268)

Here is the last charge:

> And caught their weapons clumsily,
> And marvelled how and why –
> In such degree, by rule and rod,
> The people of the peace of God
> Went roaring down to die.

> (CP 296)

Even the meditative moments are breathless, and recall the absent presence of the battle cry:

> He broke them with a broken sword
> A little towards the sea,
> And for one hour of panting peace,
> Ringed with a roar that would not cease,
> With golden crown and girded fleece
> Made laws under a tree.

> (CP 227)

These stanzas may easily be taken for noisy nonsense. Without at this stage considering what sense or otherwise they make, simply notice their noisiness. In the first stanza there is the internal echo of 'Higher' and 'higher', which further encourages the conspicuous dipthong end-rhyming of 'fire', 'higher', 'desire' and 'brier'. In the second stanza, the anaphoric 'And' generates a movement arrested with the end-stopped second line, which holds us in the suspense of its dash. When the third line starts up, it gains alliterative and rhyming pace ('rule and rod'; 'people', 'peace', 'God') before spilling over the fourth line (where all previously lines had been end-stopped) to at last make semantic and rhyming coherence of that lingering 'why –', with the 'roaring down to die'. The third stanza is more measured, appropriately so given its content, but here still there is something of the onward march, evoked by the tolling alliterations ('broke . . . broken'; 'panting peace'; 'Ringed . . . roar'; 'golden . . . girded'), suspended (and so increasingly suspenseful) syntax, and asymmetrical lineation (between six and eight syllables), which makes for a dynamic elasticity.

Notwithstanding this inclination to hecticity, Chesterton can also manage delicate metaphors. But these, too, are typically secured through the *drama* of the stanza, and only offered up with the final line and rhyme. Here is a deftly worked simile for Eldred's inner life:

> But smoke of some good feasting
>   Went upwards evermore,
> And Eldred's doors stood wide apart
> For loitering foot or labouring cart,
> And Eldred's great and foolish heart
>   Stood open like his door.

(CP 235)

He can also modulate and constellate likenesses. In the following stanza, the second, third and fourth lines give way to successive metaphors on the same idea, before that idea is dramatized in the final line, across the comma:

> There lives one moment for a man
> When the door at his shoulder shakes,
> When the taught rope parts under the pull,
> And the barest branch is beautiful
> One moment, while it breaks.

(CP 251)

Here is another example of this *eingeschachtelt* technique: a simile opens up into a metaphor, out of which emerges another simile, in just four, imaginatively coherent lines:

> But like a cloud of morning
>   To eastward easily,
> Tall Eldred broke the sea of spears
> As a tall ship breaks the sea.

(CP 280)

An interpretative context for these effects – the noisy roar and the dramatic figurative fecundity – may be found in those occasions where the ballad fails. One kind of characteristic fault may be attributed to carelessness. Where lines do not scan,[5] or metaphors do not work;[6] or, most befuddlingly, where he describes the left wings of the opposing armies facing each other in the battle of Ethandune. These blemishes are perhaps to be expected from one who wrote quickly and rarely revised his verses. There is, though, another kind of characteristic fault that is the opposite of the first: where he has taken too many pains, where he works his material too hard. Consider his paradoxical observations on the way Earl Harold dies, killed by a sword that Colan has thrown:

> And all at that marvel of the sword,
> Cast like a stone to slay,
> Cried out. Said Alfred: 'Who would see
> Signs, must give all things. Verily
> Man shall not taste of victory
> Till he throws his sword away.'

(CP 278)

The arch Christian aphorizing feels as forced as the prosody, which trips over itself at the beginning of the third and fourth lines. Moments like this remind us of how he writes best when he communicates through the atmosphere rather than the argument. That is why 'The Slaying of the Chiefs' subsection is so successful. That is also why the ballad's closing section works as well as it does. After the war has been won Alfred has a vision of 'some far century' when the heathen will come again, not with weapons this time but as reasonable-seeming secular humanists. These future scholars may come 'mild as monkish clerks' but will inspire nostalgia for open conflict, 'When pagans still were men'. There is something potentially glib if not offensive in this conceit. But before these verses are dismissed too hastily, it must be remembered how sincerely Chesterton believed in Christianity as 'a challenge and a fight':

> While it is deliberately broadened to embrace every aspect of truth, it is still stiffly embattled against every mode of error. It gets every kind of man to fight for it, it gets every kind of weapon to fight with, it widens its knowledge of the things that are fought for and against with every art of curiosity or sympathy; but it never forgets that it is fighting. It proclaims peace on earth and never forgets why there was war in heaven. (CW 2:315)

Whatever these verses are, then, they are not glib; Chesterton really believed what he was writing.[7] All the more offensive, some readers may feel. But two further qualifications need to be put. It must also be remembered why Chesterton believed in the necessity of active intolerance. 'There are two things, and two things only, for the human mind', he thought, 'a dogma and a prejudice'; a dogma is 'a definite point'; a prejudice is only 'a direction'. ('That an ox may be eaten, while a man should not be eaten, is a doctrine. That as little as possible of anything should be eaten is a prejudice; which is also sometimes called an ideal' (CW 4:48)):

41

One can meet an assertion with argument; but healthy bigotry is the only way in which one can meet a tendency... there is no force so hard to fight as the force which it is easy to conquer; the force that always yields and then returns. Such is the force of a great impersonal prejudice, such as possesses the modern world on so many points. Against this there is no weapon at all except a rigid and steely sanity, a resolution not to listen to fads, and not to be infected by diseases. (CW 4:49–50)

One final thing to bear in mind in reading these verses is that they are credible *as* verses. Chesterton does not so much argue for the reasonableness as express the conviction of Alfred's vision. The sentiment feels – that is to say, carries an atmosphere – more romantic and heroic than bigoted and bloodthirsty. In a word, the passage, and the ballad as a whole, is successful because it is successfully *dramatic*.

It has been proposed that Chesterton creates his drama at the level of the stanza; and that this drama arises not so much out of individual words, or phrases, or lines, so much as out of the complete sense – prosodic as well as semantic – that unfolds across several lines taken together. To explore this idea further, several different examples will briefly be considered; the first is from the second stanza of 'On Righteous Indignation':

> When Adam went from Paradise,
>   He turned him back and cried
> For a little flower from Paradise;
> There came no flower from Paradise;
> The woods were dark in Paradise,
>   And not a bird replied.

> (CP 184)

The almost tautologous interweaving does not further an argument; it is fixed – as the ballad as a whole is fixed – on the pain of Paradise lost. This Tennysonian technique of circling occurs here in slightly different way, in the third stanza of 'On the Downs':

> For you came out on the dome of the earth
> Like a vision of victory,
> Out on the great green dome of the earth
> As the great blue dome of the sky for girth,
> And under your feet the shires could meet
> And your eyes went out to sea.

> (CP 74)

Chesterton's control of his dramatic atmospheres becomes more remarkable as the lines of his verses become longer; such as in the penultimate stanza of 'Mediævalism':

> When the usurer hunts the squire as the squire has hunted the
>   peasant,
> As sheep that are eaten of worms where men were eaten of sheep:
> Now is the judgement of earth, and the weighing of past and
>   present,
> Who scorn to weep over ruins, behold your ruin and weep.

(CP 85)

Or as he works with large stanza units (such as in 'For Five Guilds'); or indeed when he writes verses with both long lines and also large stanza units; such as in this excerpt from 'Lepanto':

> And many a one grows witless in his quiet room in hell
> Where a yellow face looks inward through the lattice of his cell,
> And he finds his God forgotten, and he seeks no more a sign –
> *(But Don John of Austria has burst the battle-line!)*
> Don John pounding from the slaughter-painted poop,
> Purpling all the ocean like a bloody pirate's sloop,
> Scarlet running over on the silvers and the golds,
> Breaking of the hatches up and bursting of the holds,
> Thronging of the thousands up that labour under sea
> White for bliss and blind for sun and stunned for liberty.

(CP 120)

Here is another example, from the opening of 'The Last Hero':

> The wind blew out from Bergen from the dawning to the day,
> There was a wreck of trees and fall of towers a score of miles away,
> And drifted like a livid leaf I go before its tide,
> Spewed out of house and stable, beggared of flag and bride.
> The heavens are bowed about my head, shouting like seraph wars,
> With rains that might put out the sun and clean the sky of stars,
> Rains like the fall of ruined seas from secret worlds above,
> The roaring of the rains of God none but the lonely love.
> Feast in my hall, O foemen, and eat and drink and drain,
> You never loved the sun in heaven as I have loved the rain.

(CP 188)

Subsequent stanzas close with similar summative lines, each of which is a modulated echo of the one before it: 'You never loved

a woman's smile as I have loved her frown'; 'You never loved
your friends, my friends, as I shall love my foes'; 'You never
laughed in all your life as I shall laugh in death'. He realizes a
similar effect in the quietly menacing octameters of 'The Secret
People'.[8] Having stanzas prime and recall each other heightens
the atmosphere of each individually, making the verse's drama
greater than the sum of its stanzaic parts. In all these examples
quoted, we may admire the architecture of the verses and the
artisanal skill of the author. Few English poets apart from
Tennyson and Swinburne have attempted such unwieldy forms.
It is no small accomplishment to build momentum when
working with couplets (that threaten to break into discrete
two-line units), and with line-units of up to sixteen syllables
(that threaten to break into two or more discrete units within the
line itself). But it is not so much the cumulative effect as their
readerly affect which is important to notice here. The comparison with Tennyson and Swinburne is in this sense misleading.
They are better poets: they are poets. Chesterton offers something else. His verse is not without lovely localized lines and
images, but the dogma (as opposed to the 'direction') of his
writing is defined in other terms: as a dramatic rampancy, of
'rigid and steely sanity'.

When Chesterton is not roaring into battle he is often to be
found roaring with laughter, as clashed swords are exchanged for
chinking beer glasses, and seriousness for satire. His high style is
amphibiously appropriate to comic as to dramatic verse. He
employs, for instance, the same iambic heptameter couplets as
'The Last Hero' to entirely different effect in 'The Rolling English
Road', which begins with the spry beeriness, 'Before the Romans
came to Rye or out to Severn strode,/ The rolling English
drunkard made the rolling English road' (CP 203). This versatility
and humour are on full display in his 'Variations of an Air', in
which he ventriloqizes Tennyson, Yeats, Browning, Whitman and
Swinburne through their imagined re-workings of the nursery
rhyme of 'Old King Cole'. He offers a similar affectionate parody
in 'Answers to the Poets'. This series includes verses in the
manner of, among others, Browning and Swinburne, but also
those of double parody, where 'The Skylark Replies to Wordsworth (*As it might have appeared to Byron*)' and 'The Sea Replies to
Byron (*As it might have appeared to Wordsworth*)'.

Delightful and dizzying stuff: but there is a rigid and steely sanity here too. 'To a Modern Poet' is a barbed charade that sends up the 'New Movement'. The charge is of a perverted creative imagination; of making the fatal mistake of poetry that is more than half the fatal mistake about humanity: there is no simple pleasure and therefore no pleasure at all, only troglodytic sophistication expressed through calculated unmetricality:

> But I am very unobservant.
> I cannot say
> I ever noticed that the pillar-box
> was like a baby
> skinned alive and screaming.
> I have not
> a Poet's
> Eye
> which can see Beauty
> everywhere.

(CP 43)

What is most distressing is the failure to take joy even in their perversity: 'But I can't help wishing/ You got more fun out of it' (CP 44). This is pure Chesterton. Everything is approached at full tilt, which is why his verses can be so compelling. Correspondingly, however, it can sometimes be difficult to know whether he is tilting at windmills or giants, or whether he knows the difference. Especially in his early verse, he was much influenced by Swinburne's example. There are marked differences between them as writers, of course, in style almost as much as subject matter (Chesterton could never be diffuse, or debauched); but their shared taste for alliteration, suspended sense, exotic rhymes, incantatory rhythms and phrasal refrain carries with it the same danger of unwitting self-parody. Though 'he sometimes hits brilliantly at other times he misses badly' wrote Hopkins of Swinburne.[9] In a specific sense, the same applies to Chesterton. 'Nebuchadnezzar the King of the Jews,/ Suffered from new and original views' (CP 205) is obviously in the vein of Edward Lear, or Gilbert and Sullivan. What, though, of verses that begin like this?

> Five kings ruled o'er the Amorite
> Mighty as fear and old as night;

45

Swathed with unguent and gold and jewel,
Waxed they merry and fat and cruel.
Zedek of Salem, a terror and glory,
Whose face was hid while his robes were gory;
And Hoham of Hebron, whose loathly face is
Heavy and dark o'er the ruin of races;

(CP 358)

This might be funny – if it were trying to be. As it is, 'The Ballad of the Battle of Gibeon' is, simply, misconceived (it does not get any better in the hundred and twenty lines that follow). Although it was an early poem, published in 1900, as part of collection in which he later identifies 'innumerable examples' of 'errors of literature',[10] it cannot be excused as juvenilia. Verses from all stages in his life are pitted with similar 'errors'. Moreover, this early collection contains some of his most celebrated creations (notably 'The Donkey'). It is therefore better read as an excess of that which otherwise makes his best verses as good as they are. For every overworked effort like 'A Song of Gifts to God', or 'The Strange Music', there are robustious beauties like 'The Song of the Wheels', whose juggernaut progress stays just the right side of ridiculous.

His verses work best, that is, where their drama is highest without quite becoming camp. It does not matter as much as it might with another writer that a number of his pieces are topical and political. The occasion for 'Sonnet with the Compliments of the Season', say, or 'A Song of Swords' would be lost on the modern reader. Their appeal is by no means lost to history, though, because we enjoy his verses for the same reason: for the vitality of their verbalism. While the dominant poetic culture of the early twentieth century finds spring a cruel awakening, Chesterton's verses teem. This is true in the sense in which they are extraordinarily varied in subject matter. It is also true in the sense in which his verses do not vary. From the homespun happiness of 'love in English lanes' ('A Marriage Song' (CP 136)) to the slaying of dragons, or heathens; from propagandist pieces to religious devotions, to whimsical topsyturveydom: his verses may be many different things but they are all in their own ways transitive, teleological, restlessly seeking a climax.

What kind of climax is well characterized by the final stanza of 'The Wise Men'. The preceding nine stanzas are unremarkable, perhaps to throw the last into greatest possible relief. In any case, the simile that governs the final stanza makes sense of those that have come before it, as it also happens to make sense of his ebullient poetics in general. Across the opening line-break (and 'break' is the right word) his generative glee is held up for our baffled inspection:

> Hark! Laughter like a lion wakes
> To roar to the resounding plain,
> And the whole heaven shouts and shakes
> For God Himself is born again,
> And we are little children walking
> Through the snow and rain.

(CP 140)

Laughter, the least solemn and most innocent of things, proves both ferocious and feracious, the clarion of Christ's coming that, in a further inversion, enlightens wise men into childhood. There are, it seems, not two kinds of roar in Chesterton. The guffaw and the battle cry express the same conviction. When asked whether he could imagine Christ walking down the street before a brass band, Chesterton recalled the occasion when 'certain priggish disciples' rebuked street children for shouting too loudly, and Christ said: 'If these were silent the very stones would cry out.'

'With these words', Chesterton suggests, 'he founded Gothic architecture' (TT 111). The most literal meaning of this comment is that 'All Christian temples worth talking about have gargoyles', where it seems as if the very stones do cry out (TT 112). But there is a more far-reaching meaning too. By emphasizing Christ's approval of 'a natural noisiness at a great moment', and by identifying the same noisiness in Gothic architecture, Chesterton paraphrases the theological context for his idea of beauty. What 'thrills and soothes', what defines the 'soul' of the Gothic, is not its 'grandeur' but in its 'gaiety' (MM 209); that it is 'alive' and even, he fancies, 'on the march' (MM 212). Not all of Chesterton's verses bristle with spires tilted like spears. It is not necessarily even that most of his best verses are military. But all of his verses are most definitely alive. Even the least pugnacious draw on the same dramatic atmosphere; his hilarity is *hilaritas*, 'The giant laughter of Christian men/ That roars through a thousand tales' (CP 266).

47

*

Oddly enough, there is something altogether less dramatic about his drama. Although two of his nine extant plays, *The Wild Knight* (1900) and *The Turkey and the Turk* (1925), are written in verse, his writing for the stage represents an instructively different kind of thinking. It tends to be less driven by breathless narrative on the battlefield and more by wry dialogue of the drawing room. Plays suited his taste for parley; the greatest champion of Chesterton's gifts as a playwright, Bernard Shaw, specifically urges his suitability to the genre in terms of him being 'a born genius for dialogue that needs no training'.[11] And where the battles are of wits rather than brawn, where characters fight with words rather than weapons, more intricate ideas may emerge in his plays than is typical in his verse.

It is not helpful to generalize here. Reading through Chesterton's plays as a group, perhaps the most conspicuous thing about them is how remarkably unlike each other they are: from a romantic fable on free will (*The Surprise*), to a pastiche on the traditional Christmas mummer's play (*The Turkey and the Turk*), to the adaptation of one his novels (*The Flying Inn*). And yet, what does unite them is that they are most definitely written *as* plays. That is to say, the extent to which they work well or otherwise does not depend on the diversion of his established talent, as a versifier, say, or as a writer of fiction. With the partial exception of *The Flying Inn*,[12] his plays may be seen in their best light as scripts inviting a performance. This applies even to *The Wild Knight*, which is written in verse, and was published as part of a collection or verse and (no doubt for this reason) appraised by contemporary reviewers as a 'dramatic poem' rather than verse drama. Although he expressed hopes that it might be staged, it never was. A blessed relief the reader might reasonably conclude. But the theatre-goer might well feel differently. It is an extravagantly histrionic piece that seems aware of its mild absurdity (unlike, say, 'The Ballad of the Battle of Gibeon'). Moreover, its best moments are those which are most melodramatic; such as where Redfeather confronts Lord Orm: 'One touch of this bright wand [lifts his sword] and down would drop/ The dark abortive blunder that is you,/ And you would change, forgiven, into flowers' (CW 11:47). To imagine his sword a 'wand' of forgiveness that works by a 'touch'; reserving 'you' until it has first been characterized by the mixed (and tautological?) triple metaphor 'dark abortive blunder'; the deliberate tone introduced by parenthetical commas around 'forgiven': there is a richness here that is liable to be read as overwritten and overblown, but which may be enjoyed as a spectacle, as a theatrical event.

Magic is likewise shown at its best when experienced as a performance. A stranger persuades a young woman that he is a wizard. Subsequently pressed on the matter by her family, he admits he is actually a conjurer. Later still, when affording an evening's entertainment for the family, he closes with a trick that defies explanation; and this drives the young woman's brash young brother to delirium. The other characters try to persuade the stranger to explain how the trick was done, to save the young man from madness, and death. Each time he refuses. When he eventually gives way to the young woman, it is to explain that the secret of the trick would not help her brother anyway because he would not believe it. The secret of the trick is that it is not a trick, it is magic. In a final twist, the stranger must fabricate a natural explanation for the supernatural happening, to persuade the brother that he is actually only an illusionist after all.

Chesterton's retrospective verdict was that the audience ought really to have been in on the play's 'central secret' from the start, that it might have exploited the suspense and subtlety available through the use of 'Greek irony' (*CW* 11:11). Perhaps that might indeed have made for a superior theatrical experience; but as far as we may judge the play Chesterton actually wrote, its appeal rests on the very fact that we are denied such privileged detachment. In, say, *Oedipus Rex*, the 'drama' of the drama is secured through prolepsis. The tension and tragedy is inspired not by the chance, and the revelation, that Oedipus sleeps with his mother and kills his father, but by the chance revelation that he would do this, that he attempts to evade his fate, and that he yet unwittingly fulfills the gruesome prediction. Whereas in *Magic*, the play works well for the very reason that we do not know what will happen next: its suspense is not of foreknowledge but of shared ignorance with the audience with whom we meet each new turn in the story. Each twist provokes because it surprises. And what it provokes is not simply the pleasure of duck-rabbit doubleness or Russian-doll intricacy. Underneath the conversational crossfire (riding his favourite hobbyhorses, from vegetarianism to prohibition) a sustained philosophical position is established.

Given Chesterton's own early dabbling in the occult, and his subsequent religious convictions, it is tempting to read the play as a cautionary tale about the perils of spiritualism. But there is more to it than that. As a symbol of modern scepticism, the young man comes to represent the madness of modernity that must be made sane by a lie. He is the only character to fall into madness, but (with the exception of his sister) all those who seek to assist him, the doctor, the clergyman and his uncle (the Duke), share the same scepticism: none of them can believe in magic. The most telling indictment would appear to be on the materialist clergyman whom the stranger rebukes for making nonsense out of his 'coat' and 'cursed collar'. Yet the implications of the Duke's scepticism are the more damning. His principled unbelief, which has him supporting opposing causes simultaneously, is a comic motif that curdles as his moral relativism comes to be viewed as part of the same misguided madness, but worse. Compared with his agnosticism, his nephew's delirium is tacitly recommended for its commitment. As Denis J. Conlon has suggested, the play petitions 'for any kind of belief' (CW 11:98). When in *The Judgement of Dr Johnson* the judgement finally falls, it falls on this play too: Swift comes to see that he has dissipated his days, and asks what he should do with the rest of his life; Dr Johnson replies: 'Fight on the wrong side if you must; but fight' (CW 11:293).

Formally and thematically disparate as his plays may be, then, there is yet some noteworthy overlap between them. Insofar as they set faith against scepticism, and action against idle relativism, they ask to be read back into verses: as touching, for instance, those often-quoted lines from 'The Ballad of the White Horse' that refuse the pragmatic comfort of sure victory in favour of the principled certainty that a battle must be fought: 'I tell you naught for your comfort/ Yea, naught for your desire,/ Save that the sky grows darker yet/ And the sea rises higher' (CP 233). But this potted survey cannot conclude on a note that appears to link Chesterton's verse to his drama by some Panglossian inversion whereby his roar against 'pessimism' is idealized into war-mongering – and the just fight into, just, fighting. His critical writing offers the most direct and sustained critique of military muscle-flexing even when justified by an impeccably argued utilitarianism; he was a staunch opponent of British imperialism. It is hard to imagine a more perfectly poignant account of the 'heroic tenderness' of the reluctant soldier than his essay on 'The Conscript and the Crisis'. The same sympathy and intelligent scepticism is to be found in his drama too, however, as suggested by the briefest consideration of one further play; one that has been described not only as the finest example of his dramatic gifts, but also as 'the finest possible statement of Chesterton's philosophical and political position' (CW 11:52).

Published in monthly installments between October 1904 and May 1905, *Time's Abstract and Brief Chronicle* is likely the first of Chesterton's plays to have caught Shaw's eye; or rather his ear, for it succeeds solely through his 'born genius for dialogue'. There is nothing else: the only action occurs in the words. Three politicians debate. What emerges is the mess war makes of neat principles. A variety of positions are explored before the culminating question of whether it is right to wage war. Here, there is a change in tone; the philosophical, or even romantic, detachment falls away. The conversation turns against 'the mental atmosphere of the London journalist, whose ideas of war are founded on things like horse races and cricket matches'. Specifically, the debaters turn against the urge to address war (in this case, the Russo-Japanese conflict) with 'regret and respect' when it deserves our 'pity and terror'; when it should 'purify our emotions of all sentimental pollutions' (CW 11:94). In this there is, of course, reflexive irony. Chesterton writes so well against crass hack bellicism because he was himself professionally embedded within the culture, being – before and after he was anything else as a writer – a London journalist. Even in his most gung-ho balladeering, even when his roaring is all that can be heard, he remained close enough to Fleet Street to remember what Fleet Street forgets, that there is a difference between sentiment and sentimentality.

3

━━━━━━━━━━━━━━━━━━━━━━━━━━━━━━━

Essays

A paradox may be a thing unusual, menacing, even ugly – like a rhinoceros. But, as a live rhinoceros ought to produce more rhinoceri, so a live paradox ought to produce more paradoxes. Nonsense ought to be suggestive... (*CW* 29:51–4)

Chesterton spent more time writing essays than anything else. Far too much time, many of his contemporaries thought; and many subsequent readers would agree. Edmund Clerihew Bentley (of clerihew-inventing fame) regretted his old school friend's willingness to be 'bound by the iron rules as to space and time' of the newspaper contributor.[1] Chesterton's 'insistence upon the treadmill of weekly journalism after it ceased to be financially necessary seems to have puzzled his friends as much as it puzzles me' wrote W. H. Auden, before steadying himself onto the front foot: 'Whatever Chesterton's reasons and motives for his choice, I am quite certain it was a mistake' (*HC* 263). It is well to be suspicious of certainty founded on puzzlement; and the more so here, because Auden speaks as that most unreliable of critics, the sympathetic critic. He is puzzled that Chesterton did not devote himself to 'full-length books' because he specially admires his writing of that kind – just as Shaw was frustrated that Chesterton did not dedicate himself to writing for the stage. But it is no good to lament that he allowed himself to be cramped by deadlines and copy-length imposed by newspapers when the essays themselves – literally thousands of them, the majority of which were written for his weekly columns – are the opposite of cramped.

There is, Chesterton would have been the first to observe, a paradox to freedom. This is true in the general sense in which, say, the discipline of learning chords and scales may liberate a person into being able to play the piano. It is also true in the more specific sense in which the feuilletonistic form – including the attendant pressure to meet fixed copy-length and deadlines – provided creative conditions particularly hospitable to his exploratory way of thinking.[2] He is not being as ironical or as hard on himself as it might seem when he admits he has 'only too good reason to know' that 'if you are writing an article you can say anything that comes into your head' (*TT* 148). A professional licence to write pabulum released him from all obligations but his afflatus. The appeal of his essays is aesthetic, and the authority to which they appeal is aleatory: however ingeniously rationalized, his arguments do not ultimately depend on empirical proof or logical reasoning but on unexpected and chance connections.

'The essay is', he observes, 'the only literary form which confesses, in its very name, that the rash act known as writing is really a leap in the dark'. That is not to say the genre is unable to do responsible work. On the contrary, he is staking a kind of Kierkegaardian necessity in the leap of faith where darkness demands it. The 'misleading air of responsibility about the Essay is very disarming through appearing to be disarmed'; and he concedes the danger to mislead that comes with this. But he must also conclude that the best essays are so good precisely because the essayist has not been 'obliged to set forth his thoughts...in the theses of a medieval schoolman' (*CW* 35:41;45). The 'whole atmosphere' of the genre is, he says, 'full of doubt, experiment and effort'.[3] Auden and others miss this when they emphasize Chesterton's closeness to the aesthetes of the 1880s and 1890s who aimed to be 'continuously "bright" and epigrammatic' (*HC* 263–4). Because of its speculative ambition the essay may go further, or find itself in more interesting places than other kinds of writing. Chesterton's essays are indeed bright and epigrammatic – but they are not *continuously* so; and on this distinction turns a great deal. They work from light to shade, from humour to seriousness; and not clumsily or chaotically; the movement is deliberate: it is the moment where they 'leap'.[4]

While he draws on a number of standard rhetorical devices, the defining character of his argufying is altogether more opportunistic and less respectable than the hard-won syllogistic triumph. Even where he approaches the classical mode, he

53

typically appeals to a literary rather than logical authority. Where he attempts *reductio ad absurdum*, for instance, he inevitably finds more absurdity than the expedient proof by contradiction. Here, to take another device, is the Chestertonian version of *a fortiori*, the truth value of which depends not on binary-logical proposition but on metaphor:

> It is a weakness to fail in feeling that a statue standing on a pedestal above a street, the stature of a hero, carved by an artist, for the honour and glory of a city, is, so far as it goes, a marvellous and impressive work of art. But it is far more of a weakness to fail in feeling that a hundred statues walking about the street, alive with the miracle of mysterious vitality, are a marvellous and impressive work of God. (*AG* 162)

If the atmosphere of Chesterton's essays may therefore be called subjective and aesthetic, his favoured method might be called the *semi-sequitur* surprise. Through various kinds of analogical thinking – puns, similes, metaphors and, of course, paradox – he grants abstract ideas shape and substance, and pushes these ideas into unexpected relationships. For him: 'Thinking means connecting things' (*CW* 1:238); and 'laughter is a leap' (*CW* 1 :326). *Mental Leaps* is the title of a recent book in cognitive science that anatomizes 'analogy in creative thought'. Chesterton launches himself in ways that go unimagined by such scientistic taxonomies. Here is an example of his thinking through puns:

> Tyranny is the opposite of authority. For authority simply means right; and nothing is authoritative except what somebody has a right to do, and therefore is right in doing. (*AW* 158)

In its first use 'right' means 'correct'; in its second, it means 'entitlement'. The third use imbricates the previous two, and draws down the complementary associations of what is 'considered proper, correct or consonant with justice', and also, 'something proper for, or incumbent on, a person to do' (OED). Given his ideological sympathy with the Middle Ages, it seems likely that Chesterton has in mind here the medieval synonymity of 'civil law' with 'civil right'. What his opposition between tyranny and authority exposes is that tyranny means the opposite of civil rights and is therefore itself the opposite of what is right. Tyranny is – by paronomastic proof – shown to be wrong.

Sometimes he couches his analogies with delicate provisionality (*'Perhaps* this modern simplification in political symbols *might* be compared not only to the simplification in science but to the simplification in art' (*GS* 77; emphasis mine). Other times, we are urged to take his analogues unexpectedly far ('But what most people do not see is that this dullness in diet, and similar things, is *exactly parallel* to the dull and indifferent anarchy in manners and morals' (*AW* 40; emphasis mine). When we are not being prepared in this way, we may find that a leap has already been made, and we learn of it in terms of what has been left behind:

> That is why the traditional art is the only truly creative art. That is why it is more truly creative than the negative abstractions which tend, of their nature, not merely to anarchy, but to nothingness. And that is why a glimpse of these things encouraged me in my own lifelong belief in particularism, and the tales and traditions of a people (*AS* 25).

Or the leap may be more like a triple-jump:

> In the world of ethics this is called liberty; in the world of economics it is called property. And in the world of aesthetics, necessarily so much more dim and indefinable, it is darkly adumbrated in the old dramatic unities of space and time (*FF* 97).

The importance of surprise to his method is suggested in his essay 'On Sightseeing', where he reflects on the effectiveness of monuments 'set up purposely in order to be seen accidentally'.[5] Surveying the 'striking tower on a hill, an arresting statue on a pedestal, a remarkable relief over an archway, or any other piece of public art' that is actually 'intended for the traveller, and even especially for the chance traveller', he explains:

> It was meant for the passer-by, perhaps in the hope that he would not merely pass by; perhaps in the hope that he would pause, and possibly even meditate. But he would be meditating not only on something that he had never seen before, but on something that he had never expected to see. The statue would almost spring out upon him like a stage brigand. The archway would arrest him and almost bar his path like a barricade. He would suddenly see the high tower like a sort of signal; like a rocket suddenly sent up to convey a message, and almost a warning. (*AG* 164)

55

This is, he says, the way many popular monuments have been seen; it is also 'pretty much the best way to see them', because: 'No man will ever forget the sights he really saw when he was not a sightseer' (*AG* 164). When he writes in his *Autobiography* that the only 'real advice' he could give to a 'young journalist' would be 'to write an article for the Sporting Times and one for the Church Times and put them in the wrong envelopes', the serious part of his half-serious comment is that: 'What is really the matter with almost every paper, is that it is much too full of things suitable to the paper' (*CW* 16:177). The hope that the passer-by might not pass by, that he might pause, and possibly even meditate; that is the hope he extends to his essays too. There is something more substantial to this than the journalistic anxiety of keeping impatient thumbs from page-turning. The virtue of surprise is pragmatic without being purely aesthetic: it connects with his mystical ambition – which is also a hard-headed political ambition – to show the world in its true strangeness, for its ugliness and its beauty.

In an eristic piece exposing the way big shops drive little shops out of a business, he creeps up on his subject. One opinion is offered as a way of introducing 'another and much more curious truth'; namely, that the 'vulgar and insolent' 'monster' emporiums not only lie about their inevitable superiority, they boast about their bluff being a bluff. They express pride, that is, in the success with which they manipulate the psychology of the shopper into believing their shop and their goods to be superior. This bluff can and should be called, Chesterton insists, 'before the last traditions of property and liberty are lost': by shoppers, simply, shopping elsewhere. But if we do not pass too quickly by this essay, if we pause and possibly even meditate on its significance, another level of indirect meaning emerges. The essay is not primarily about shops at all, it is about people. The central complaint and curiosity is that 'it never occurred to anybody to resent' 'the mere mad stampede towards monopoly'. What Chesterton finds most surprising, and what his essay above all attempts to redress – by surprising the reader into seeing it – is that 'Nobody seemed sufficiently alive to be annoyed' (*CW* 5:87–8).

These essays sometimes aim to annoy, sometimes to delight;

often both.[6] But they always work by the same principle: of saying something surprising enough, or in a surprising enough way, to roust the reader into life. In this sense, he writes with the same 'ingenuity' he admired in William Cobbett: because he 'has not struck any attitudes of a demagogue or a prophet of woe', the reader 'does not know what is coming; but when it comes it comes to *him* and not to some remote stranger': he 'surprises us from the inside' (*WC* 217–8). Part of the justification for his method of surprise is reflexive, that he himself found the world consistently startling. Many of his essays are indeed no more than a re-telling of his epiphanies. In 'The Advantages of Having One Leg', he ruminates on his sprained foot: 'This world and all our powers in it', he comes to see, 'are far more awful and beautiful than we ever know until some accident reminds us' (*TT* 42). 'The Architect of Spears' is an account of 'an optical illusion' that 'accidentally' revealed 'the strange greatness of Gothic architecture' (*MM* 208). In 'The Romance of Rhyme', having conceded that 'it is of course only an accident that Horace opens his greatest series of odes by saying that he detests the profane populace and wishes to drive them from the temple of poetry', he nonetheless suggests that 'it is the sort of accident that is almost an allegory' (*FF* 15).

Accidents may, it seems, accidentally reveal what ratiocination cannot. There are essays 'that are really themes and themes that are really theses': 'They represent what may be called the Extreme Right of rigid right reason and militant purpose, after the Latin model'.[7] Chesterton preferred those 'very English' essays that are 'none the less beautiful because they twist and ramble like an English road'.[8] His ideas suddenly emerge on the horizon, or round the corner, without warning; by chance.

Occasionally he drops his analogical *aperçu* as soon as it comes to him. More often, he runs away with it. His essay on 'The Fallacy of the Umbrella Stand' begins with the idle suggestion that a 'Socialist' 'means a man who thinks a walking-stick like an umbrella because they both go into an umbrella-stand'. He draws his figure out over several pages of close argument, leaping this way and that. The obscure, hardly serious seed of an idea grows into something of unexpected scale and sophistication. And, importantly, it is not only the reader who is surprised. The argument as it develops confounds his own initial estimation of that 'curtly' expressed and 'careless simile'.[9]

Something must now be said about his use of paradox. A good reason not to open a discussion on Chesterton's style by considering paradox is that most critics who do so never get on to anything else. This is as true for those who defend as those who deride it. Because the former tend to take his paradoxes as the philosophically respectable exception to his style, and the latter, as the epitome of what is philosophically disreputable in his style. It is here argued that his paradoxes should be seen in a third category: as the epitome of what is philosophically significant in his writing style. This *tertium quid* looks back to the introductory chapter: to read Chesterton right it is necessary to see that his paradoxes are the fullest expression not of his 'wit', but of his 'humour'.

When he published his first collection of essays, *The Defendant*, the reviewer for *The Academy* spoke for many in judging that: 'The wheels of his matter skid under the energy of his thinking, the result being much steam but little motion.... His energy is great, but it does not move or lift. Invited, as we imagine, to see him swim the Hellespont, we discover that we are only privileged to see him splash cleverly in his bath.' Described as Chesterton's 'natural device', paradox is said to be the most conspicuous symptom and cause of the problem, being adopted 'as a means of laying a train of epigrammatic gunpowder with time fuses carefully adjusted' (*CJ* 36–7).

'Epigrammatic' damns the faint praise of 'gunpowder' and 'carefully adjusted'; it connects his prose to the attitudinizing Auden associates with the aesthetes. Chesterton's rhetoric may be pyrotechnically impressive – fun, even dangerous – but (it is argued) when the dust settles its impact is 'crude and juvenile'. Chesterton 'has the poetic gift of expressing his ideas unexpectedly so that they come home with a sudden thrill', and this enriches his verses (*CJ* 36). When it comes to his essays, however, this same gift blows the gaff on their epistemological paucity. What enhances one genre proves incompatible with another: 'prose stands for what it is, and the judicious reader insists on organic and purposeful thought' (*CJ* 37). A 'judicious reader', it is implied, demands judicious *thinking*. Here is the rub. It is taken as self-evident that paradox is by its nature philosophically 'crude and juvenile'. Shadowing this assumption is a superstition that the only way to say serious things on serious subjects is by being serious. What follows is an attempt to show the error of both these positions.

Kenner's *Paradox in Chesterton* demonstrates that there may be good and bad paradox, just as there is good and bad art; it also shows that what makes paradoxes good and bad varies. 'There is', Kenner explains, 'a metaphysical use of paradox that answers to the complexity of being, especially the Supreme Being, and a rhetorical use that answers merely to the complexity of human folly'. In the former type, 'the intrinsic contradiction is not in the words but in the things' (*PC* 16–7). (More recently, Yves Denis makes the same distinction and presses the same case, though he prefers the terms 'pedagogical' versus 'doctrinal' paradox).[10] Having made this distinction, Kenner seeks to disentangle the practical joker from the 'practical mystic' (*PC* 142); and he does this with considerable sophistication. It is hard to resist the conclusion that 'Chesterton must be taken seriously because paradox must be taken seriously, both as a tool of expression and as an ingredient in reality' (*PC* 5).

And yet, Kenner's scrupulous disregard of Chesterton's artistry, his thoroughgoing attempt to isolate 'the essential' from 'the auxiliary' in his writing (*PC* 3), is too crude to convince. It is not clear how a qualitative distinction can be made between paradox and other 'devices' such as, say, catachresis, with which it is continuous, and of which Chesterton is almost as fond. Even if paradox is granted as a special case, it remains to be shown how different instances of its use may be identified as being either 'essentially verbal' or 'essentially metaphysical' (*PC* 16–17). Aidan Nichols makes the point that 'in both instances the literary techniques employed are similar: a build-up of argumentation or persuasive discourse is suddenly concentrated in a phrase that shocks'; and so, the difference 'is not itself stylistic'.[11] The difference is, rather, a matter of the ontological disclosure a certain kind of paradox offers.

But the question of disclosure is not as straightforward as it might seem either. Humour is an important part of the way paradox discloses; but humour may also be constitutive of what is disclosed: because paradox works paradoxically. If it is true that 'Chesterton must be taken seriously because paradox must be taken seriously', it is also true that Chesterton must be read

59

for his humour because paradox must be read for its humour. Less obvious but no less important is that Chesterton must be taken seriously because paradox must *not* be read seriously. Henri de Lubac describes paradox's 'realm of election' to be 'the life of the spirit'. In that sense, it is metaphysical. In describing how paradox makes its appeal to the life of the spirit, however, de Lubac emphasizes its aesthetic identity; he describes it as playful and suggestive rather than didactic or dogmatic. Paradoxes 'make sport of the usual and reasonable rule of not being allowed to be *against* as well as *for*'.[12] This 'sport' 'has more charm than dialectics'; 'it is also more realist and more modest, less tense and less hurried'. The paradoxical quality of paradox is, in short, its charismatic confidence in certain ontological and mystical antinomies expressed through an 'anxiety to avoid a certain doctrinal heaviness when serious things are being dealt with'.[13]

Considered for its ambition to handle the heaviest matters with the lightest touch, paradox is metonymic of Chesterton's entire argumentative method. Although he aligns himself with the 'very English' essay, he is in this respect closest to what he admires as the achievement of French literature and philosophy: 'the supreme and splendid triumph of looking shallow, and being deep' (*CI* 221). The way Chesterton's essays 'leap' – and, crucially, the reason we as readers leap with them – is determined by their atmosphere. What allows them and us the courage to leave the *terra firma* of 'rigid right reason and militant purpose', of 'organic and purposeful thought', is their acknowledged 'doubt, experiment and effort'. The modern philosopher is, he says, 'like a sort of confidence man' who asks us to accept assumptions that offend common sense; 'he will straighten out the world, if once he is allowed to give this one twist to the mind' (*CW* 2:514). By contrast, Chesterton's arguments appeal to the same authority as Thomist philosophy, to 'the mind of the man in the street' (*CW* 2:514). This authority may often be invoked retroactively, after the mind has been twisted to see the world straight. Moreover, his *semi-sequiturs* may serve as more than a perspectival wrench: they may be the argument itself. In his essay on 'The Toy Theatre', he writes:

> Has not everyone noticed how sweet and startling any landscape looks when seen through an arch? This strong, square shape, this shutting off of everything else is not only an assistance to beauty; it

is the essential of beauty. The most beautiful part of every picture is the frame. (*TT* 150-51)

What applies here to the way beauty is framed applies also to the way in which (rhetorical) beauty may itself serve as a frame. Once again, the device of paradox brings the matter into focus. The way paradox frames its subject is not merely an assistance to thought, it is the essence of its thinking. The point is easily missed; as, for instance, Žižek demonstrates when he writes that 'the limitation of Chesterton' is 'his not being Hegelian enough'.[14] Having asserted that 'the proximity of his theological paradoxes to Hegelian dialectic cannot fail to strike us',[15] Žižek presumes it cannot fail to strike us, either, that dialectics is the dialectical refinement of paradox – something that Chesterton could have seen for himself if only he had taken his paradoxes to their full paradoxical conclusion. But this is shoddy reasoning. Žižek fails to notice the 'atmosphere' in which paradox operates – its charm, its modesty, its lightness of touch – and therefore fails to see why it is 'less tense and less hurried' than dialectics. He fails to see, that is, the very 'function' of paradox which is 'to remind the dialectician when each new stage is reached in the argument, that however necessary this forward movement is no real progress has been made'.[16] Another way of saying the same would be to notice that paradox may be paradoxical in its 'substance', but also, as de Lubac suggests, paradoxical in its 'rhythm':

> When we discover it and hold it in our hands we do not have time to bring our first look of satisfaction to rest upon it before it has already fled. The eternal story of the Pharisee starts afresh in each of us. To get hold of the elusive truth again, we should perhaps seek it in its opposite, for it has changed its sign. But often we prefer to hug its rotten corpse. And we go rotten with it.[17]

So it is that those 'theological paradoxes' Žižek thinks proximal to Hegelian dialectics are nothing of the kind. They do not promise progress through mutual correction. Chesterton's most urgent use of paradox is indeed to emphasize how the founding principles of his faith are aporetic: to press the elusiveness of their 'elusive truth'; to explain why he feels 'especially proud of those parts' of his religion that are 'most commonly called superstition' (*CW* 16:85). For related reasons, he is suspicious of

61

what he calls the 'fatal metaphor of progress, which means leaving things behind us', because it 'has utterly obscured the real idea of growth, which means leaving things inside us' (as the 'heart of the tree remains the same, however many rings are added to it' (*FF* 2)).

What has been said here of his paradoxes may be broadly applied to his writing in general. Namely, that it is necessary to resist the Pharistic, which is also the Philistinic, interpretative impulse. The atmosphere of his writing cannot be dismissed as adventitious; how he argues defines what he is arguing. In support of this, three main observations have so far been made: that his essays are 'full of doubt, experiment and effort'; that this expresses itself through an accidental kind of leaping logic; and that this expression is epitomised by his use of paradox. A fourth and final characteristic of his essay style will now be explored, one which provides a fuller context for appreciating the other three. If his thinking tends towards paradox rather than dialectics, and is therefore concentric rather than progressive, his essays also move in a way that he calls 'centripetal'. He argues that the best literature, and indeed the best of the worst literature, expresses itself in this way. 'What is true of a Shakespeare play is equally true of the shilling shocker':

> The shocker is at its worst when it wanders, and escapes through new scenes and new characters. The shocker is at its best when it shocks by something familiar; a figure or fact which is already known though not understood ... I am delighted when the dagger of the curate is found to be the final clue to the death of the vicar. But there is a point of honour for the author; he may conceal the curate's crime, but he must not conceal the curate. I feel I am cheated when the last chapter hints for the first time that the vicar had a curate. I am annoyed when a curate, who is a total stranger to me, is produced from a cupboard or a box in a style at once abrupt and belated. I am annoyed most of all when the new curate is only the tool of a terrible secret society ramifying from Moscow to Thibet. These cosmopolitan complications are the dull and not the dramatic element in the ingenious tales ...
>
> In short, the good mystery story should narrow its circles like an eagle about to swoop. The spiral should curve inwards not outwards. And this inward movement is in true poetic mysteries as well as mere police mystifications.

(*FF* 95)

This passage may inform our reading of Chesterton's own 'ingenious tales', by encouraging our attention to their specifically 'dramatic element' (which is a different but not entirely unrelated quality to the 'drama' the previous chapter locates in his verses). We may enjoy his stories with a renewed admiration for the way they surprise us with what we already know. It is necessary to recognize how central is this conceit to his literary works before it can be recognized how important is the same dramatic element in his non-fiction. Not that Chesterton imports an effective 'literary' technique into his essays for ornamental appeal. It is truer to say that he experienced life and regarded his faith as a mystery consistent with the tallest of his stories. 'What we call' the 'triviality' of life is, he explains, 'really the tag-ends of numberless tales; ordinary and unmeaning existence is like ten thousand thrilling detective stories mixed up with a spoon' (*TT* 9). The 'thrill' to which he refers has been located so far in certain localized moments where his arguments leap. What has not yet and will now be explored is the wider movement, where the irrelevance and triviality of his accidental, tangential method is redeemed: where he *swoops*.[18]

But first, a caveat. In his account of Dickens's great characters, Chesterton notes that it is 'impossible to do justice' to them, because 'the essential of them is their multiplicity'; their 'whole point' is that he 'made them by myriads', 'that he stamped his foot and armies came out of the earth' (*CW* 15:185–6). The same must be said of Chesterton's essays. No single essay, no single collection of his essays – indeed, no collection of collections – is as remarkable as the thousands he never preserved in separately published works after they had seen light for a single day in his newspaper column. They are so many, so good and written for sufficiently different audiences that even the most generous selection looks meanly arbitrary. Without therefore the delusory hope of coverage, what follows is a look at two essays that offer an earnest of his signature swoop.

'A Piece of Chalk' recounts his attempt to do some chalk drawing on brown paper. His plan is frustrated because he has left the white chalk, the 'most exquisite and essential chalk, behind'. But then he realizes that, being in Sussex, the landscape is made 'entirely out of white chalk'; so he stops and breaks a piece off a rock he is sitting on and uses that. This précis records where the essay's narrative goes, but not how it gets there. What is missed out is the 'dramatic element' which is the essay's defining element. Partly, it is a matter of tone. The essay begins like this:

> I remember one splendid morning, all blue and silver, in the summer holidays, when I reluctantly tore myself away from the task of doing nothing in particular, and put on a hat of some sort and picked up a walking stick, and put six very bright-coloured chalks in my pocket. (*TT* 1)

Doing nothing in particular is wryly described as a 'task' from which he must tear himself away; but to what? In the casual piling up of clauses as much as in the vagueness of 'a hat of some sort' and the juvenile associations of 'six very bright-coloured chalks', there is a similar but elevated purposiveness without purpose. That first adjective, 'splendid', stretches out across the whole sentence as a gesture of self-witnessing pleasure: the morning is splendid, so are the summer holidays, so is everything about his proposed artistic adventure that the morning and the holidays invite. The subsequent exchange with a 'very square and sensible old woman' who owns the house accentuates this splendidness, by contrast. She assumes he must want brown paper for its obvious use (wrapping parcels), and then for a less obvious use (as inexpensive note-paper); so he must explain that he does not want to use the paper as a means to an end but as an end in itself, because he simply likes 'the quality of brownness in paper, just as he likes 'the quality of brownness in October woods, or in beer, or in the peat-streams of the North':

> Brown paper represents the primal twilight of the first toil of creation, and with a bright-coloured chalk or two you can pick out points of fire in it, sparks of gold, and blood-red, and sea-green, like the fierce stars that sprang out of the divine darkness. All this I said (in an off-hand way) to the old woman; and I put the brown paper in my pocket along with the chalks, and possibly other things. I suppose everyone must have reflected how primeval and how poetical are the things one carries in one's pocket; the pocket-knife, for instance, the type of all human tools, the infant of the sword. Once I planned to write a book of poems entirely about the things in my pocket. But I found it would be too long; and the age of the great epics is past. (*TT* 2)

The deadpan parenthesis of the second sentence acknowledges that the fantasia of the first is overblown. It is funny. But it is not frivolous. What brown paper 'represents' is consistent with the way he uses it. He was not 'going to sketch from nature', he was 'going to draw devils and seraphim, and blind old gods that men worshipped before the dawn of right, and saints in robes of angry crimson, and seas of strange green, and all the sacred or monstrous symbols that look so well in bright colours on brown paper' (*TT* 3–4). His is an authentic account, in other words, of how he sees brown paper – in comedic contrast to the old woman's strict sense of its utility.

That he 'possibly' put other things in his pocket along with the paper and chalk feeds another punch-line, which comes with what he pretends to 'suppose' in the next sentence. Again, though, his case for the 'primeval' and 'poetical' contents of pockets that would take great epic verse to describe is not pure silliness. As he shows in 'What I found in my pocket' (an essay published in the same collection (*Tremendous Trifles*, 1909)), the conceit invites further symbolic and spiritual suggestions. It is important to expect, and to enjoy, this relentless irrelevancy. Even where we may, like the sightseer, pause and meditate on his disporting profundities, it is often unclear how fervently he intends each gesture. And because there are so very many such gestures, expressed with such fluency, the narrative always draws the reader on. The next paragraph beckons with an analogy of how the 'colossal contours' of the Sussex downs on which he walks 'express the best quality of England, because they are at the same time soft and strong': 'The smoothness of them has the same meaning as the smoothness of great cart-horses, or the smoothness of the beech-tree; it declares in the teeth of our timid and cruel theories that the mighty are merciful' (*TT* 3).

The subsequent three paragraphs contain light-but-earnest speculations on how poets and artists may engage and express the natural world. Then, calm horror: he realizes he is missing white chalk. A lengthy paragraph diverts to 'the wise and awful truths which brown-paper reveals'; namely, 'that white chalk is a colour', and 'not a mere absence of colour'. He finds 'moral significance' in this revelation, for the analogy it presents: that virtue is not, either, the absence of vice but itself a 'vivid and separate thing' (*TT* 5). After a theological detour via Joan of Arc and the frock coats of city gentlemen comes a pin to prick this philosophical balloon: 'Meanwhile, I could not find my chalk'.

The essay concludes with 'a sort of despair', him staring 'stupidly round', until, with a swoop, everything resolves: he suddenly sees that the whole grand peninsula of the south of England is one giant piece of chalk. This final joke at his expense – he describes himself as a man in the Sahara unable to find sand, or, mid-ocean, unable to find salt-water – comes, in the finest tradition of the detective tale, with the shock of 'something familiar; a figure or fact which is already known though not understood'. 'Then I suddenly stood up and roared with laughter, again and again' (*TT* 6–7). There would be no equivalent bathetic relief without the previous wild and whimsical, aesthetic and spiritual raptures on brown paper and white chalk which prepares this moment. That is the drama, and what makes him and his readers laugh so heartily.

One final example: 'The Little Birds Who Won't Sing' opens with some thoughts on Gothic carving, and how 'vigorous' are its representations when compared with the composure of the gods and heroes carved by the ancient Greeks (*TT* 195–6). The representation of trades and toils and tradesmen toiling is, he argues, eloquent of social and religious differences between the cultures. Ruskin had by this time already made (and lost) a career on reading moral and social lessons into art and architecture.[19] But Chesterton goes further. Looking at these carvings he is struck by a peculiarity of which he cannot be sure about their 'curious heads'. He wonders if they are singing.

Typically, he is less concerned with whether they really do depict men singing than with the truth that singing is connected with many of the tasks being depicted. On his way home he sees some men working in the fields, and he notes that there are still songs for harvest and for many agricultural routines. He also happens to hear some sailors singing in chorus and in different songs according to what part of their work they are doing. And so, 'suddenly', he wonders why 'it should be quite unknown for any modern trade to have a ritual poetry' (*TT* 197). If there are songs for reapers and for sailors hauling ropes, why might auditors not sing while auditing and bankers while banking? He tries out some specimen verses.

Predictably, hilariously, he is rebuffed. A bank clerk advises him of 'an indefinable something in the very atmosphere of the society in which we live that makes it spiritually difficult to sing in banks' (*TT* 199). But then, unexpectedly, the swoop; irony at the expense of the ingenuous Chesterton is traduced into a penetrating social and spiritual critique. There are arresting moments in Chesterton's essays; he is the master of the filigreed sentence, and it is for his breviloquence that he is best known. His one-liners are eminently quotable. But it is in the way his essays 'leap', and most of all in the way they 'swoop', that his most significant thinking is to be found. One way of describing this dramatic quality is to say he lays 'a train of epigrammatic gunpowder with time fuses carefully adjusted'. Except that his arguments are not linear. They are 'centripetal'; they recur and recoil and reimagine themselves, by reaching beyond themselves. 'Great poets', he suggests, 'use the telescope and also the microscope' (*AC* 275). His greatness as an essayist is that he uses the microscope as a telescope. This is better shown than told. Here is how 'The Little Birds Who Won't Sing' ends, where the essay's title is at last engaged and interpreted in the very last sentence: the previous riff on the significance of song assumes a new symbolism; the secular and the spiritual, the human and the super-human, are brought together:

> And the more I thought about the matter the more painfully certain it seemed that the most important and typical modern things could not be done with a chorus. One could not, for instance, be a great financier and sing; because the essence of being a great financier is that you keep quiet. You could not even in many modern circles be a public man and sing; because in those circles the essence of being a public man is that you do nearly everything in private. Nobody would imagine a chorus of money-lenders. Every one knows the story of the solicitors' corps of volunteers who, when the Colonel on the battlefield cried 'Charge!' all said simultaneously, 'Six-and-eightpence.' Men can sing while charging in a military, but hardly in a legal sense. And at the end of my reflections I had really got no further than the sub-conscious feeling of my friend the bank-clerk – that there is something spiritually suffocating about our life; not about our laws merely, but about our life. Bank-clerks are without songs, not because they are poor, but because they are sad. Sailors are much poorer. As I passed homewards I passed a little tin building of some religious sort, which was shaken with shouting as a trumpet is torn with its own tongue. THEY were singing anyhow;

and I had for an instant a fancy I had often had before: that with us the super-human is the only place where you can find the human. Human nature is hunted and has fled into sanctuary. (*TT* 200–1)

4

Biography

> What is wanted in modern biography is something as simple as the single line that marks the sweeping curve or the sharp corner in a weather-chart; or that yet more simple line that runs round the nose or chin in a caricature. (*WC* 57)

It has been said that Chesterton's biographies are really always about himself. That is unfair; though there is something buried within the aspersion which touches an important truth. He saw most clearly those virtues in other people that were his virtues; he could also be blind to those virtues he did not share, or believed to be vices. There are occasions where his judgement amounts to bigotry, such as when he figures Thomas Hardy as 'a sort of village atheist brooding and blaspheming over the village idiot' (*CW* 15:483).[1] For the most part, however, his anamorphic estimation of those qualities he did or did not share with a subject renders these qualities with an instructive clarity. Because they are exaggerated, we see them more truly. Hyperbole is in him a kind of hypostasis. Consider the grandiose panoptic with which he closes his book on Bernard Shaw:

> I know it is all very strange. From the height of eight hundred years ago, or of eight hundred years hence, our age must look incredibly odd. We call the twelfth century ascetic. We call our own time hedonist and full of praise and pleasure. But in the ascetic age the love of life was evident and enormous, so that it had to be restrained. In an hedonist age pleasure has always sunk low, so that it has to be encouraged. How high the sea of human happiness rose in the Middle Ages, we now only know by the colossal walls that they built to keep it in bounds. How low human happiness sank in the twentieth century our children will only know by these extraordinary modern books, which tell people that it is a duty to be cheerful and that life is not so bad after all. Humanity never produces optimists till it has ceased to produce happy men. It is strange to be obliged to

impose a holiday like a fast, and to drive men to a banquet with spears. But this shall be written of our time: that when the spirit who denies besieged the last citadel, blaspheming life itself, there were some, there was one especially, whose voice was heard and whose spear was never broken. (*BS* 109–10)

All of his books, and most of his individual chapters and essays conclude with an efflorescent whirl of this sort, a distillation and an extension of what has gone before. The argument suddenly grows in scale and becomes more vivid in its colouring, more dramatic in its appeal. It is a seductive and satisfying experience. His books are worth picking up for their conclusions alone. Read the final paragraph of *What's Wrong With the World*, or of *Orthodoxy*; or indeed that of, say, *The Everlasting Man*, or *William Blake*, or *Saint Francis of Assisi*. His summative sentences represent some of the finest prose he ever wrote; which is to say, they represent some of the finest prose in the English language. Read them. Except that their full effect cannot be felt by reading them on their own; they need to be understood as the drawing together and re-expression of the hundreds and thousands of sentences to which they are responding. The whole work finally takes flesh, or rather takes flight, with a force of momentum.

The paragraph quoted above is, however, a rare example where his conclusion seems to be at odds with its premises. It is not an accurate account of Shaw; it is not even an accurate account of his own biography of Shaw. What it is, and brilliantly so, is a melodramatization of his own life's work, driving men to live vital lives: the medieval Merry Englander with his spear tilted against modernity. He never again describes himself so well, even in his *Autobiography*.

Shaw inspired men away from pessimism. But Shavian optimists are, Chesterton regrets, 'sometimes rather pallid optimists, frequently very worried optimists, occasionally, to tell the truth, rather cross optimists…they can exult though they cannot laugh' (*BS* 109). His disciples endure all the pagan pleasures with a Christian patience: 'Let us eat, drink and be serious' (*BS* 101). More important even than his Irishness, Chesterton urges us to understand that 'Bernard Shaw is a Puritan and his work is Puritan work' (*BS* 63). The 'first spirit in Puritanism' he describes as 'a refusal to contemplate God or goodness with anything lighter or milder than the most fierce concentration of the intellect. A Puritan meant originally a man whose mind had no holidays' (BS 20). And later: 'There is at least one outstanding fact about the man we are studying; Bernard Shaw is never frivolous. He never gives his opinions a holiday' (BS 21).

Unequivocally, then, here is a man more sympathetic to imposing a fast than imposing a holiday like a fast. Shaw's essential severity is, Chesterton invites us to see, especially evident when he is apparently least serious, when he is most witty. He 'can endure lawlessness but not levity' (BS 23); because 'his wit is never a weakness', 'it is never a sense of humour': 'he does not see things suddenly in a new light; all his brilliancy is a blindingly rapid calculation and deduction'; 'he never said a thing that he was not prepared brilliantly to defend. He never breaks out into that cry beyond reason and conviction' (BS 21). This idea is revisited and elaborated in every chapter. Shaw's optimism is 'a serious optimism – even a tragic optimism'; he 'follows the banner of life; but austerely, not joyously' (BS 84); for him, 'life is a thing too glorious to be enjoyed' (BS 46). He is, in other words, nothing like the smiling stalwart with the unbroken spear who is transfigured at the end of the book. His ferocious, tenacious and ingenious turning of scepticism against the sceptics invites the idea of a man with a dangerous weapon: it is just that he did not use it to urge men to holidays and banquets. That man was Chesterton.

Shaw coined the name 'Chesterbelloc' to describe Chesterton's close personal and political partnership with Hilaire Belloc. But it was Chesterton's biography of Shaw that yielded a weirder, wittier chimera: the 'Shawterton'. Shaw has his tongue firmly in his cheek when he suggested that Chesterton's biography was 'the best work of literary art I have yet provoked' (CJ 201). But his irony is outdone by Vivian Carter's review in The Bystander in September 1909 (CJ 210–1), which is the most amusing review that a work by Chesterton has ever provoked. Carter opens with the revelation that there is actually no such man as G. K. Chesterton, that he is an opportunistic invention of Bernard Shaw. Because Shaw had grown weary of Socialism, teetotalism and vegetarianism, he invented an antithetical alter-ego to ridicule his defining –isms. This remarkable deception has been made possible, Carter explains, by Shaw having taken up residence close to the tunnel connecting the Adelphi with the Strand. Leaving his house 'plain, Jaeger-clad, bearded and saturnine', he would enter his tunnel, in a cleft in which was a cellar, remove his false beard, don an immense padding of chest, a sombrero hat and coat and pince-nez, before emerging into the Strand – to feast on the forbidden joys of Individualistic philosophy, meat food and strong drink. This can be the only explanation for the biography now issued: that the book is 'wholly spurious', a desperate last play by Shaw to forestall the exposure of his dual identity.

It is very well done; almost a nod to Chesterton's own creative experiments with double-identities (especially to those duplicities of *The Man Who Was Thursday* published just the year before). But Carter's review also happens to be entirely wrong. The reason she finds the book to be 'a bad biography' is worth noticing for the same reason that Chesterton quotes a critic describing Stevenson as an epigone for Poe (*CW* 18:52–7). Carter's conclusion as to what is 'bad' in Chesterton's biography is worth noticing because it is 'so astonishingly untrue' that it suggests the truth which is its opposite. Carter thinks Chesterton reduces Shaw to the accident of his Irish birth, his religious ancestry and such habits of mind as mathematics and music. As a study of a person, the biography is therefore 'strangely analytical'; 'shorn of its paradoxical pyrotechnics', it reads 'like a proposition of Euclid'; it is 'all premises, and demonstrations, and corollaries.' In short, the 'human Shaw does not breathe in these pages' (*CJ* 211).

Chesterton's prefatory comments suggest the reverse ambition. In considering Shaw's 'relation to the stage', he explains, 'I am going to write of three soils or atmospheres out of which that relation grew'. It should be clear enough by now that what Chesterton means when he writes about 'atmospheres' is nothing like Euclidian logic. He addresses the generic facts of Shaw's life – that he is Irish, Protestant and Progressive – precisely because he wants to get past these facts. It is a necessary, if also (he concedes) clumsy strategy of refining 'conventional phrases' into a meaningful narrative.

Of course, readers may feel Chesterton interprets these 'atmospheres' wrongly; and this is a delicate matter on which to adjudicate. There may be something blunt and condescending in the notion that the 'fierce fastidiousness' of Shaw's vegetarianism is 'one of the allotropic forms of the Irish purity' (*BS* 12); or, that if he lived 'for three hundred years, he would be a Catholic' (*BS* 114). Yet, there may be something subtle and significant in the related ideas that he was a vegetarian 'more because he dislikes dead beasts than because he likes live ones'; and that, 'However he may shout profanities or seek to shatter the shrines, there is always something about him which suggests that in a sweeter and more solid civilisation he would have been a great saint' (*BS* 11).

Chesterton's judgement may be variously judged, but it must at least be according to what he was trying to do. In an extra chapter written for the republished 1935 edition, he makes a jibe at the 'good and faithful biographer'. This he is not, and never was. He presumes more intimacy with his subjects, while paying correspondingly less heed to the facts of their lives, or even to their own account of their life and work. He has 'not the slightest intention' of accounting for everything Shaw wrote, because he is 'much too interested in what he really means to bother...about everything he merely says' (*BS* 112–13). Carter knows there is nothing in the joke that Chesterton is Shaw's creation and that this biography is an attempt to preserve the illusory difference between them. But what she does not see is that Chesterton has here created Shaw by an illusion that blurs the differences between them. To suggest the Shawterton might actually exist is more edifying than a joke whose punch-line carries punch only if Chesterton is presumed to be Shaw's antithesis. Chesterton exaggerates, but what he exaggerates is a deeper truth than what he denies, about an affinity between the men more instructive than their differences.[2]

The limitations of Chesterton's biographical and literary critical approach are therefore clear. As his brother, Cecil, described it, he is 'at his best when he is analyzing a writer with whose root point of view he is sympathetic'.[3] Although he and Shaw differed, he finds their points of view converge at 'root'. Where he cannot find such sympathy, however, he can find nothing; or what was for him worse, he finds nihilism. Because he comes to believe all roads lead to Rome, he cannot imagine that alternative philosophies offer anything but blind alleyways.

He is too Catholic to be catholic. It is tedious to read, for instance, his erroneous assertion that Walter Pater died a Catholic (*CW* 15:450), or his speculation that Shakespeare lived as one.[4] Why, in an ostensibly literary biography, is it necessary to make a detour defending the orthodoxy of Chaucer's faith? Some critics have found it hard to see what – other than a certain *partis pris* satisfaction of claiming the best men for your own team – is at stake in such 'ecclesiastical haggling' (*CJ* 493). But Chesterton explains his position often and openly: 'It is enough to say that with other creeds they would have been, for literary purposes, other individuals' (*CW* 15:423).

If there is, then, a limit to Chesterton's taste, it is not in the end all that limiting: because his faith expresses his Catholic creed, and not the other way round. As will be discussed in the next chapter, his theology is an emphatically *emotional* response to life rather than dry dogmatism. In any case, he wrote most about those with whom he felt the most sympathy. The obvious exception here is *The Victorian Age in Literature*, which has marvellous localized insights to recommend it – many believe it to be one of his finest works – but it differs from his other book-length studies for requiring him to evaluate subjects across an historical period whose closing decades were for a him a byword for decadence and pessimism; and he cannot do it. But this book stands apart in its unevenness. He achieves a imaginative empathy in his biographies of Cobbett, Browning, Stevenson, Blake, Watts and St Francis of Assisi. His studies of Chaucer, Dickens and St Thomas Aquinas are especially to be noted for the way (*contra* Carter) his subjects are made to 'breathe in these pages'.

Chesterton identifies a 'secret hero-worship which is the heart of biography' (*RB* 7). This is no kind of secret when it comes to his own work. He confesses his affection on every page. Partly, he is consciously reacting against the 'new fashion of minimising and finding fault' (*CW* 18:41). But he is equally conscious that honest praise must not be heedless. Like God 'in the great saying of a Scottish mystic', he thinks the 'good critic' should be 'easy to please and hard to satisfy' (*FF* 16). If he falls short of Arnoldian disinterestedness, his partiality allows him to see the best in his subjects and their work, but also the best in the worst, and indeed the worst in the best.

Chesterton's first critical study was on Robert Browning, in which he petitions for a method that would define all his subsequent studies. He is wary of the springes of scholarship; he suspects that the facts may not be enough, that they may even get in the way. The special 'sin and snare of biographers' is 'that they tend to see significance in everything; characteristic carelessness if their hero drops his pipe, and characteristic carefulness if he picks it up again' (RB 5). The 'great temptation of this kind of work' is 'the noble temptation to see too much in everything' (RB 6). He is not simply advocating circumspection. Simultaneously, he is arguing for greater scrutiny of those things too insubstantial and subjective to qualify as facts. The 'most practical duty of biography' is, he says, 'also the most difficult': 'to catch and realise and put upon paper that most nameless and elusive of all things – social tone':

> We do not want to know about a man like Browning, whether he had a right to a shield used in the Wars of the Roses, or whether the tenth grandfather of his Creole grandmother had been white or black: we want to know something about his family, which is quite a different thing. We wish to have about Browning not so much the kind of information which would satisfy Clarencieux King-at-Arms, but the sort of information which would satisfy us, if we were advertising for a very confidential secretary, or a very private tutor. (RB 5)

So it is that the entire biography turns on the suggestion that, 'About the time of Browning's boyhood a very subtle and profound change was beginning in the intellectual atmosphere of such homes as that of the Brownings' (RB 14). We cannot understand Browning until we understand that he was born into 'the age of inspired office-boys', and 'in the atmosphere of literary youth, fierce and beautiful, among new poets who lived in a new world':

> It is important to remember this, because the real Browning was a quite different person from the grim moralist and metaphysician who is seen through the spectacles of Browning Societies and University Extension Lecturers. Browning was first and foremost a poet, a man made to enjoy all things visible and invisible, a priest of the higher passions. (RB 16)

These comments on atmosphere are sufficiently capacious –

which also means sufficiently contradictory – to make sense of the whole portrait of man and poet; from 'the particular character' of his love for Italy (*RB* 82) and for Italian art as 'the love of a living thing' (*RB* 85), to his 'ardent and headlong conventionality' (*RB* 100). There can be no appreciation of the *sui generis* in any of his subjects, nor in their achievements, he suggests, until something generic is first appreciated about the atmospheres in which they lived. 'Splendid as is the art of [G. F.] Watts technically considered', 'we shall misunderstand his work from the outset' unless we understand what it means that he was 'deeply committed to, and so unalterably steeped in' the atmosphere of the early Victorian period (*GW* 7). 'It is useless for us to attempt to imagine Dickens and his life unless we are able at least to imagine this old atmosphere of democratic optimism – a confidence in common men' (*CW* 15:47). That, moreover, his historical period was an 'atmosphere of popular optimism' (*CW* 15:48); and that he, personally, enjoyed as a boy 'an atmosphere of perpetual applause'; that, therefore, 'there did mingle with his merits all his life this theatrical quality, this atmosphere of being shown off – a sort of hilarious self-consciousness' (*CW* 15:53).

Where his subjects are at furthest remove, historically and culturally, he expends greatest effort to make these foreign atmospheres present and felt. His book on Chaucer opens with familiar abnegations. 'It makes no claim to specialism of any sort in the field of Chaucerian scholarship'; 'It does not in any of the disputed details, dictate to those who know much more about Chaucer than I do' (*CW* 18:151); and so on. Chesterton is not giving away his authority as a biographer and critic, he is establishing his own, different terms for that authority. He does not look to scholarship but to himself. He has 'a personal conviction that the poet could be an extremely popular poet' combined with having 'felt suddenly the fierce and glaring *relevancy* of all the walking social symbols of the Chaucerian scene to the dissolving views in our own social doubts and speculations to-day'. 'Feeling this so strongly', he explains, 'I simply could not force myself to the usual stiff official attitude of dealing with all such things as dead' (*CW* 18:152).

The chapter devoted to 'The Age of Chaucer' does not therefore chart a conventional historical narrative: 'medieval history is useless unless it is modern history' (*CW* 18:180). It is not possible to have a personal response to Chaucer's writing until a personal response has been established with 'the peculiar rich autumnal atmosphere of the Chaucerian epoch' (*CW* 18:192), especially the 'the religious atmosphere of the time' (*CW* 18:183). His book on St Francis proceeds in the same way. 'To any one who can appreciate atmospheres', he writes, 'there is something clear and clean about the atmosphere of this crude and often harsh society' into which St Francis was born (*CW* 2:44). His chapter on 'The World St. Francis Found' draws together the extended account of 'the spirit of the time', 'the penance that followed paganism':

> While it was yet twilight a figure appeared silently and suddenly on a little hill above the city, dark against the fading darkness. For it was the end of a long and stern night, a night of vigil, not unvisited by stars. He stood with his hands lifted, as in so many statues and pictures, and about him was a burst of birds singing; and behind him was the break of day. (*CW* 2:45)

Out of context, these comments on atmosphere are likely to sound vague and unconvincing. The last quotation is an example of where he attempts to make something abstract into something concrete, to make the generic singular: where he tries to make his atmospheres atmospheric. Metaphors of darkness, fading darkness, and then twilight; before the burst of bird-song, and daybreak: there is both substance and rhythm to this spiritual backdrop against which St Francis would raise his hands.

Perhaps the paragraph is, in the end, too picturesque to be evocative. He generally does better by going further in the transformation of his descriptions into dramatizations: real (or at least reported) actions or events in the life or works of his subjects are isolated as being in some wider sense emblematic. Having 'come to a sort of understanding' with the girl who was to become his wife, William Cobbett 'solemnly placed in her hands a sealed packet of money, telling her to use it whenever she was in need'. When his regiment crossed the Atlantic, 'she was lost in the poverty of a modern town'. On his return, after much searching he at last tracked her down 'to a slum where she was working as the poorest sort of servant; and she handed him back his packet of money with the seal unbroken'. What this 'small gesture of repayment' meant for Cobbett was something 'as splendid as the throwing of a gauntlet'. It is, Chesterton suggests, 'very significant of Cobbett's career from its earliest days' (WC 42). 'To enter into his sense of triumph', though, 'we must understand something that is found in him through life, and especially found in him, when it is generally rarest, in youth'. A considerable digression on this 'something' follows, and is then acknowledged in this way: 'I have dwelt on this one case...because it is something very near to the whole secret of the man's life' (WC 45).

It is through such representative moments that Chesterton takes hold of his subjects. Rather than attending democratically to all the possibly relevant evidence, he seizes on a few choice details; often the most unpromising details. The 'clinging curse of all criticism of Chaucer' is 'the fact that while the poet is always large and humorous, the critics are often small and serious': 'they not only get hold of the wrong end of the stick, but of the diminishing end of the telescope; and take in details when they should be taking in a design' (CW 18:159–60). By contrast, Chesterton does not fill in the picture from the inside, he goes straight for the outline. 'A book like this can be but a bare outline of a life so full as that of William Cobbett'; 'Nevertheless an outline is needed; and is an outline that is not often supplied. It is the advantage of such a small scope that it can focus what often seems formless and sprawling, through being too large to be seen.' (WC 57)

Form is given to formlessness, facts are ordered into outline by his standing back from his subjects. This is a different thing from calculating their whole as the sum of the (necessarily incomplete) collected facts. 'Cobbett produced a vast and voluminous mass of work; and vast and voluminous masses of work have been produced about Cobbett. Most of it is interesting and much of it is true; but none of it is the truth.' Or put another way: 'There have been caricatures enough of Cobbett; but they caricatured the wrong features. They missed the point. The subject of Cobbett has been admirably amplified; but when it has been simplified, it has been simplified wrong' (WC 57–8).

Quite what it means to 'simplify right' is suggested by his apology for the technique of exaggeration in Dickens's fiction, which may be read as an apology for his own exaggerated claims about Dickens's person. Whereas events in Cobbett's early years display 'something *very near* to the whole secret of the man's life', in 'The Youth of Dickens', Chesterton finds that '*the whole secret* of his after-writings is sealed up in those silent years of which no written word remains' (*CW* 15:66; emphasis mine). This seems not to allow for the adult Dickens to be anything other than the child of his childhood; and in this sense it over-determines the argument. Which brings us back to Carter's criticism. But like the best caricatures, it also clarifies; as the example of Dickens's characters shows so well:

> If any critic depreciates the ... method as mere overstatement, the answer is obvious: let him take some of these ... people and overstate them. He will soon realize that it is not a simple matter of exaggeration, in the sense of mere extension. It is not a matter of making a man a little taller or a morning a little colder; the challenge to the imagination is not whether he can exaggerate, but whether he can find anything worth exaggerating. (*CW* 15:567)

In other words, like Dickens, Chesterton's portraits may tend towards the two-dimensional; but also like Dickens, they are curiously alive for that very reason: because he tends to 'exaggerate life in the direction of life' (*CW* 15:89). He does not flatten out his subjects, he distils them. Or at least, he distils something in them to which he responds most strongly – usually, because he is responding to something in himself. It is something more like cathexis than transference. His response to Robert Louis Stevenson, for instance, is organized round a single idea, an idea that happens to be at least as applicable to the biographer as to his subject; and he certainly exaggerates its significance. The governing idea of Chesterton's biography of Stevenson is that everything there is to know about his life and work – everything that is admirable in it, anyway – may be traced to his childhood experience of playing with a toy theatre, 'the mysterious Mr. Skelt of the Juvenile Drama' (*CW* 18:58). Chesterton describes the toy theatre as the toy 'of all toys' that has 'most of the effect of magic on the mind' (*CW* 18:58).

That playing with a toy theatre as a child may shape the creative imagination is ratified by his own experience (as documented in his *Autobiography*, his essay on 'The Toy Theatre', and elsewhere). And that is why he is able to glimpse its unique significance. But he has not imposed the idea; Stevenson has written about the influence himself. Moreover, there is in the end no need to accept the psychological speculation that 'there is at the back of every artist's mind something like a pattern or a type of architecture' (CW 18:53). Nor is it necessary to accept that what was always at the back of Stevenson's mind was Mr Skelt. These things may or may not be true; but the truth of Chesterton's argument about Stevenson's life and work does not depend on them being true. It is the other way around. 'I propose to review his books with illustrations from his life', explains Chesterton, 'rather than to write his life with illustrations from his books' (CW 18:48).

Whatever effect the toy theatre may have had on Stevenson's creative imagination, it is a symbol of something for which there is, in a sense, too much evidence. Stevenson's childhood toy reduces the man and his work to a scale that can conveniently be seen: it has been simplified right. That all Stevenson's images 'stand out in very sharp outline; and are, as it were, all edges'; that his descriptions are not only 'clean-cut', but also coloured in a way that is 'conspicuously clear and bright'; that his 'Highland tales have everything Scotch except Scotch mist' (CW 18:54–5): the supposed continuity between his early experience of cutting figures out of cardboard and his later writing career is not a cursory correspondence. It is explored by Chesterton, with illustrations of representative moments across Stevenson's work, over the ten chapters of his biography. And what emerges is more than a stylistic symmetry; his philosophy – specifically, his morality – as a writer also finds its corollary, if not its cause: 'and there was never any name for it but his own name of Skeltery' (CW 18:58).

The examples of representative moments given so far have been drawn from childhood and appear to identify happenings that are both exceptional and etiological, moments on which the lives of these subjects turn. Chesterton was chary of sounding 'like a parody of the pedantic fancies about juvenile psychology and early education' (CW 18:57). He acknowledges the hazard of reading people backwards, of seeing 'signs of them long before they begin to appear on the earth, and, like some old mythological chronicler, claims as their heralds the storms and the falling stars' (RB 7). For this reason, his representative moments are often trivial and emblematic. He goes after symptoms as much as causes. He is not so much interested in the environment in which his subjects lived so much as how they lived *against* their environments. His subjects stand out like silhouettes.

During her life and after her death, friends, fellow-poets and critics clamoured to excuse Elizabeth Barrett's *Sonnets from the Portuguese* (especially their unorthodox rhymes) as an expression of her physical debilitation. Speculation on the relationship between disease and desire in their figurative and formal structure is a critical commonplace. Mary Russell Mitford is only the most famous of those to wonder whether her isolation at Wimpole Street had led to an overly narrow experience with proper pronunciation of English. By contrast, Chesterton underscores the 'intolerable violence and more intolerable tenderness' she suffered as a way of commending how *little* it explains her life and work. That she was not made 'thoroughly morbid and impotent'; that she remained 'high-spirited'; that she was 'full of that silent and quite unfathomable kind of courage'; that 'she took a much more cheerful view of death than her father did of life' (*RB* 61): this is, for Chesterton, the overwhelmingly significant interest. And that we might take the point immediately, he pins it to an apparently inconsequential habit of opening her mail, which he takes as representative of her whole habit of being:

> Silent rooms, low voices, lowered blinds, long days of loneliness, and of the sickliest kind of sympathy, had not tamed a spirit which was swift and headlong to a fault. She could still own with truth the magnificent fact that her chief vice was impatience, 'tearing open parcels instead of untying them'; looking at the end of books before she had read them was, she said, incurable with her. It is difficult to imagine anything more genuinely stirring than the achievement of this woman, who thus contrived, while possessing all the excuses of an invalid, to retain some of the faults of a tomboy.
>
> Impetuosity, vividness, a certain absoluteness and urgency in her demands, marked her in the eyes of all who came in contact with her. In after years, when Browning had experimentally shaved his beard off, she told him with emphatic gestures that it must be grown again 'that minute'. There we have very graphically the spirit which tears open parcels. (*RB* 61)

Some of the most original and interesting work on Elizabeth Barrett's poetry today involves a de-emphasis of her infirmity, and a corresponding re-emphasis of her agency. Margaret M. Morlier, for instance, has convincingly argued that her 'rhyming experiments indicate subversive and elitist poetic strategies', which 'serve, on the one hand, to protest the traditions of beauty and of literature from which the feminine voice had been excluded and, on the other, to distinguish a more cognitively complex poetic form than popular verse'.[5] What has in literary criticism only very lately been granted – that Barrett Browning's sedentary physical state expressed itself as a subversive psychological strength – Chesterton grasped intuitively, because he rejected the 'premisses, and demonstrations, and corollaries' of the settled view in favour of the 'human' subject before him.

The refinement of Chesterton's technique of dramatizing representative moments comes where these moments recur as motifs. This is a variation on what, in discussing his essays, was called his 'centripetal' method. His book on Aquinas presents a fine example. We are introduced to the very opposite of St Francis: 'a huge heavy bull of a man, fat and slow and quiet; very mild and magnanimous but not very sociable; shy, even apart from the humility of holiness; and abstracted, even apart from his occasional and carefully concealed experiences of trance or ecstacy' (CW 2:422). Where these commonplace adjectives come to life is when they find a context. With the flair of the practised mystery writer, Chesterton describes the unexpected outcome of Aquinas's decision to become a Dominican Friar. He is kidnapped by his own brothers who shut him up in a castle. Aquinas accepts imprisonment with his 'customary composure'; 'through a great part of that strange abduction', writes Chesterton, he had been carried about 'like a lumbering stone statue' (CW 2:453–4). But this picture of placidity only sets the scene for what follows. Not long into his confinement, something happens to make him 'angrier than he ever was before or after'. His brothers introduce into his room 'some specially gorgeous and painted courtesan, with the idea of surprising him by a sudden temptation, or at least involving him in a scandal'. We are not given Aquinas's actions but his *actio*:

In this one flash alone we see that huge unwieldy figure in an attitude of activity, or even animation; and he was very animated indeed. He sprang from his seat and snatched a brand out of the fire, and stood brandishing it like a flaming sword. The woman not unnaturally shrieked and fled, which was all that he wanted; but it is quaint to think of what she must have thought of that madman of monstrous stature juggling with flames and apparently threatening to burn down the house. All he did, however, was to stride after her to the door and bang and bar it behind her; and then, with a sort of impulse of violent ritual, he rammed the burning brand into the door, blackening and blistering it with one big black sign of the cross. Then he returned, and dropped it again into the fire; and sat down on that seat of sedentary scholarship, that chair of philosophy, that secret throne of contemplation, from which he never rose again. (CW 2:454)

Powerful as it is, Chesterton does not leave the event as a localized emblem of Aquinas's character. He draws the metaphor of this flaming sword through the whole book. Aquinas's subsequent theological quarrel with Siger of Brabant sees him 'once more fighting his enemies with a firebrand' (CW 2:476). And later again, in considering his philosophical relationship to Aristotle, the metaphor returns as a compacted pun explaining why his apparent heresies never made him appear like a heretic:

It was precisely because his personal Catholicism was so convincing, that his impersonal Aristotelianism was given the benefit of the doubt. He did not smell of the faggot because he did smell of the firebrand; of the firebrand he had so instantly and instinctively snatched up, under a real assault on essential Catholic ethics. (CW 2:492)

The emotional drama of these scenes is not merely emotional in the sense of sentimental, or sensational. Something more than passion is at stake. In this case, the figure of the firebrand is witness to 'the isolated apocalypse of anger' but it also bound up in his attempt to convey the complex theological conflict that precipitates that anger. This he manages through the same technique of exaggeration and simplification, by establishing a representative moment. Framed in the conditional, Chesterton risks travesty. 'If there is one sentence', he says, 'that could be carved in marble, as representing the calmest and most enduring rationality of his unique intelligence, it is a sentence which came pouring out with all the rest of this molten lava'; 'If there is one phrase that stands before history as typical of Thomas Aquinas....' (CW 2:476)

Never mind which phrase and sentence; the point here is a more general one. The way that he makes manageable, and stirring, Aquinas's complex theology exemplifies a method he applies to the ideas and works of all his subjects (as, for instance, when he takes just two lines of verse to 'express all that is best in Blake and all that is best in all the tradition of the mystics' (*BK* 147)). It is a method that owns its own inadequacy; that announces itself as an outline, even a caricature. He is aware of his own artistic subjectivity and ideological bias, and he presumes its authority; but his criticism is more than an echo-chamber for Wilde's 'whispers of a thousand different things which were not present in the mind of him who carved the statue or painted the panel or graved the gem'.[6] He does not disregard facts, but neither does he let them stand alone: he presumes to read the facts as expressing (or disguising) a deeper pattern. *If* Aquinas may be typified in a phrase, *if* his ire may be an emblem of his unique intelligence: *insofar* as the sentence and the phrase could *ever* serve in this way, then, he says, this quotation does.

Such provisional, modal reasoning was observed in his essays as thinking through *semi-sequiturs*; it allows him to leap further. He is scornful of those 'elaborate cloacan researches' which are the scholar's warrant (*CW* 18:68–9). And scholars repaid the compliment. What needled academics most was not that Chesterton could get empirical matters wrong, but that he did so blithely. Dickens's 'shortest postcard is often as good as his ablest novel', begins Chesterton's account of Dickens's gift of 'original creation'. An early reviewer objected that the first postcard did not appear in Britain until three months after Dickens's death.[7] But Chesterton was unrepentant and the reason is that his suggestion is not, in the end, a statement of fact; it speaks to a larger truth about Dickens's creative talent which remains symbolically true, however empirically false. There is 'something that is in history or biography a great deal worse than being false', he suggests: being 'misleading' (*RB* 5). What defines Chesterton's biographies is something both less and more than the 'good and faithful biographer'. He is less interested in the brass tacks of how his subjects lived, he is more interested in the atmosphere of their imaginative lives and how these can be made to live for the reader.

5

History

Finally, a truth is to be remembered which scarcely ever is
remembered in estimating the past. It is the paradox that the past
is always present: yet it is not what was, but whatever seems to have
been; for all the past is a part of faith. (CW 20:440)

When on 14th November 1906 William James mounted the
lectern at the Lowell Institute in Boston, his audience knew
what to expect. His work as a psychologist and philosopher was
prolific and celebrated; his scholarship was almost as well-
known as the fiction of his younger brother, Henry. But the
pioneering polymath of Harvard yard was yet capable of
surprising the assembled. They had come to hear his thoughts
on 'The Present Dilemma in Philosophy'; they had come to
glean the wisdom of a venerated professor. He cleared his
throat, and what he gave them was G. K. Chesterton:

> In the preface to that admirable collection of essays of his called
> 'Heretics,' Mr. Chesterton writes these words: 'There are some
> people – and I am one of them – who think that the most practical
> and important thing about a man is still his view of the universe. We
> think that for a landlady considering a lodger, it is important to
> know his income, but still more important to know his philosophy.
> We think that for a general about to fight an enemy, it is important
> to know the enemy's numbers, but still more important to know the
> enemy's philosophy. We think the question is not whether the
> theory of the cosmos affects matters, but whether, in the long run,
> anything else affects them.'[1]

Perhaps James wanted to set an informal tone by opening with
words from one who was at this time known primarily as a
London hack with a side-line in pulp fiction. In any event, he
clearly believed that Chesterton's remarks provided a useful
way into his subsequent argument ('I think with Mr. Chesterton

in this matter', he continues). It is the argument of this chapter that James's lecture also happens to provide a useful way back into Chesterton. Specifically, James's thoughts on how that 'most practical and important thing about a man' is formed may illuminate the perverse possibility that Chesterton often appears most confused, careless and contrarian where he aims to be most coherent, deliberate and sincere.

At the heart of James's philosophical pragmatism is the conviction that neutrality and objectivity are impossible in any absolute sense. Chesterton agrees that 'apparent objective truth is not the whole matter; that there is an authoritative need to believe the things that are necessary to the human mind'. At the same time, he wants to affirm that 'one of those necessities is a belief in an objective truth' (CW 1:249; 21:255). Coming from a man with 'the almost invariable capacity, when throwing buns in the air, to catch them in his mouth' (HC 364), this may look like he is trying to have his epistemological cake and eat it too.[2] But there is no greedy contradiction here. Chesterton's pragmatism held the inevitability but also the authority of subjectivity, including its authority to know what was objectively true. This paradoxical proposal reverberates through this writing; and it is never felt more keenly than when it is apparently most inappropriate. The previous chapter touched on his tendency to privilege subjectivity and to read atmospheres over empirical data. This tendency is so much more conspicuous in a narrative that is predominantly historical rather than biographical, where the object of interest is not a person but a period. There is a *prima facie* difference, a generic distinction, between the study of a personality and the historical narrative; the latter being more directly accountable to the objective world. At least, the reader might expect there to be such a difference and distinction. That is not in any case what the reader finds in Chesterton.

A Short History of England, *The Everlasting Man* (which offers an 'historical rather than theological' view (CW 2:141)), and *The Resurrection of Rome* refuse the presumed objectivity of the traditional historical treatise. These are history books untroubled by historical dates. (Only *A Short History* contains any dates at all, it only has four, and they carry no interpretative weight.) Chesterton's casual attitude to chronology is only the most obvious way in which his histories are unusual. The introductions to these books that disclaim any 'swagger of sham scholarship'[3] do not propose caprice. They are not apologies for being insufficiently methodical; they are an apologia for a different method. Cobbett was an 'amateur historian', explains Chesterton, in the sense that 'he used his own wits': 'Those who sniff at such amateur history are not using theirs. They say the amateur's views cannot be correct, because they are not founded on research. In other words, they say he cannot see what is there, because he sees what is obviously there' (WC 169).

'The difference' between the amateur and the professional historian, he elsewhere suggests, is 'not about the facts but about the importance of the facts'.[4] His phrase offers a double confession. It speaks first of all to his belief in 'the reasonable right of the amateur to do what he can with the facts which the specialists provide' (CW 2:141); the right, that is, to interpret the same facts in a different way. But the phrase also proffers something more controversial and more central. Namely, his belief that objectivity is not necessarily desirable. It is in his histories, which demand greatest disinterestedness, that he insists most strenuously on the need to privilege perception over empiricism. That is what he means when he says the 'real past' of a people is a less pressing consideration than 'their real memory' (CW 20:440). That is why he claims 'Arthur is more real than Alfred' (CW 20:439), and Shakespeare's Henry V is 'a more important person', 'more historic' even, than the actual historical person of that name (CW 20:500). That is the reason he cares less about the actual events than what he calls 'the *inner emotions* of [for instance] the Crusade' (CW 20:467). When he contends that 'popular prejudice is generally more worthy of study than scholarly sophistry' (CW 20:528), he does not present the possibility of scholarship that is not sophistic. That is not because he thinks scholarship mere sophistry; it is because he does not think popular prejudice mere sciolism. The very fact of its popularity makes it at least true to what most people think. Or as he elsewhere puts it:

> Real history, if there could be such a thing, would not consist of what men did, or even what they said. It would consist far more of the mighty and enormous things they did not say. The assumptions of an age are more vital than the acts of an age. The most important

sentence is the sentence that a whole generation has forgotten to say; or felt it needless to say. (*CW* 21:446)

It is just such a history that Chesterton attempts to provide, a 'subjective side of history, which may more simply be called the inside of history': 'what it felt like'. Forsaking 'what is defined or deduced merely from official forms or political pronouncements' in favour of those neglected, unofficial sources, he eavesdrops on the sedimented gossip of folklore, art, architecture and literature.

The second chapter of *The Resurrection of Rome* opens by reading the statuary of St Peter's not (according to the commonplace) as frozen music, but as 'frozen rhetoric' (*CW* 21:300). A certain 'vivacity' in Italy and in the Italian spirit gives a context, Chesterton suggests, for the 'posturing' of the pontiffs. The Popes of Rome are 'orators in stone, and all this sculpture is rhetorical sculpture'. The idea is treated at considerable length. He begins by objecting to Macaulay's poetical suggestion that the ancient Greek stone sculptures breathe and struggle. This description does not fit the Venus of Milo, objects Chesterton; it does not even fit the trampling horsemen and wrestling centaurs of the Elgin Marbles. What he thinks it does accurately characterize is the sculpture of Rome. Even the Papal Tombs, 'though they deal with holy and hoary men dead and at rest in the Lord...exhibit them alive with thunderous brows and hands uplifted as if with thunderbolts; as positive as despots, as passionate as demagogues':

> The stone breathes and struggles and breaks out into great cries almost audible down the ages; for these are the statues of the sacred orators of Italy; the speakers of the Word that is given *urbi et orbi*; the men who spoke as princes to the city and as priests to the world. 'If these were silent the very stones would cry out.' (*CW* 21:303)

The argument gathers momentum over dozens of pages. At its centre is the historical moment when Pope Gregory III challenged the authority of Constantinople by excommunicating the Iconoclasts and reclaiming Rome as the head of the Christian Church. Chesterton stresses the sheer audacity of Pope Gregory's action, 'the huge disproportion that seemed to exist between the broad daylight of the Empire and the faint shadow in the West'. He tells of how the great Greek Emperor,

Leo the Isaurian, called a Council of the Church, which supported the Imperial view; and of how, without blinking, the Pope condemned the Council. Paraphrase destroys the performative power of the narrative; it must be read to feel its full pressure (and pleasure). Here therefore is an extended excerpt. Notice the urgent use of symmetry, repetition and delay through massively suspended syntax. As ever, his argument must be read aesthetically. His rhetoric is the fiery complement to the frozen oratory he seeks to describe; he ratifies by dramatizing the divine authority ossified in the fabric of St Peter's.

> The Emperor had on his side councils and colleges and the bishops of big cities, and the whole tone and talk of society and the prestige of the past and the promise of the future. The Pope had on his side deserted streets and barren provinces and frontiers broken by barbarians and the support of rude and uncertain tribes; the Pope had on his side savagery and stupidity and ignorance and desolation; and the Pope was right.
>
> He was right thoroughly; he was right a thousand times; he was right by the creative Christian principle, in which the devil cannot make but only mar; he was right equally by every modern test or taste in beauty and the liberty of the arts; he was right against the Caesarian fad of flat portraits as much as against the Moslem monomania of monotheism; he was right by the whole power and spirit of the wide culture that was already dawning darkly behind; he was as right as the oldest gargoyle of Chartres or the last statuette of Cellini; he was right with the unconscious prophecy of all that has here covered him with the flamboyance and splendour of Rome; and he was right when everyone else was wrong. Realize only that one forgotten fact about that one obscure Pontiff; and then come back to consider afresh, with what detachment and independence you will, the impression that first puzzled you; the impression that this temple of St. Peter is built to assert rather the firmness and authority and even audacity of its hierarchs than their softness or simplicity or sympathy as holy men. Realize that for many millions of mankind, including those who made this city and this shrine, it is really true; the same thing that happened in the matter of the Iconoclasts has happened again and again; and in the awful silence after some shattering question, one voice has spoken and one signal has saved the world. Never mind whether you believe this or not; fully and fairly realize that they believe it; and *then* for the first time you will be at the beginning of all comprehension of such a statuary and such a dome. (*CW* 21:325–6)

To ask why St Peter's 'is not the place where we come nearest to the charity and burning tenderness of the Heart of Christ'; why it is not designed 'to express that element of twilight and reverent doubt'; why it is 'almost oppressive in its hanging curves'; and why 'so many dead Popes hang above us thunderously like judges or point suddenly like accusers': these are the questions that must be asked of Rome, suggests Chesterton (CW 21:326). And these Rome answers in the rhetoric of every stone of its statuary that is today so difficult to hear. What the very stones cry out is 'the Certitude of Rome' and 'the Spoken Word', for which its now peacefully dead Popes were the orators and judges once 'terribly alive' (CW 21:327). That is the most important sentence once needless to say but which now needs to be said before anything may be understood.

Many and varied silent witnesses are given voice elsewhere in this book and in his others. They range from England's romantic legends of its chivalrous past to its changing attitudes towards top-hats and trousers (CW 20:439–43;578–9). For the way he eschews the most obvious evidence, it can occasionally feel as if he has spent too much time with his unconventional detectives. But what he said of Aquinas's method may be applied to him also: 'He did not, like a modern specialist, study the worm as if it were the world; but he was willing to begin to study the reality of the world in the reality of the worm. His Aristotelianism simply meant that the study of the humblest fact will lead to the study of the highest truth.' (CW 2:471)

Above all, Chesterton's sense of a subjective history must be animated by the humanity of its subject: of the men and women who lived it. So it is in writing *The Everlasting Man* he suggests that 'if this story cannot start with religious assumptions, it must none the less start with some moral or metaphysical assumptions, or no sense can be made of the story of man' (CW 2:186). To understand the history of mankind, in other words, what must be understood first and foremost is the condition of man. This applies even if the man being spoken of is the prehistoric cave-man. 'We are always told without any explanation or authority that primitive man waved a club and knocked the woman down before he carried her off': 'But on every animal analogy, it would seem an almost morbid modesty and reluctance, on the part of the lady, always to insist on being knocked down before consenting to be carried off' (CW 2:159).

When Chesterton concludes that 'there is nothing whatever in the atmosphere of the cave to suggest the bleak and pessimistic atmosphere of the journalistic cave of the winds, that blows and bellows about us with countless echoes concerning the cave-man' (CW 2:162), his conclusion in favour of the cave-man is at the expense of the contemporary man. The whole 'confusion and misunderstanding' is explicable in terms of 'a very modern mood of anarchy' (CW 2:163). He does not share this mood; he reads what little evidence there remains from the cave-man – their cave-paintings – and he gasps at how civilized they must have been. 'So far as any human character can be hinted at by such traces of the past, that human character is quite human and even humane' (CW 2:162).

There is a winning episode a couple of chapters later, when he comes to the origin of writing. In the art of hieroglyphics, 'there seems to be serious indication that the whole high human art of scripture...began with a joke'. 'There are some who will learn with regret that it seems to have begun with a pun' (CW 2:198). Picture writing necessarily requires approximation and analogy, he explains. And so, 'if people must write romances of ancient Egypt (and it seems that neither prayers nor tears nor curses can withhold them from the habit)', they should 'describe the scene of the great monarch sitting among his priests, and all of them roaring with laughter and bubbling over with suggestions as the royal puns grew more and more wild and indefensible. There might be another scene of almost equal excitement about the decoding of this cipher; the guesses and clues and discoveries having all the popular thrill of a detective story' (CW 2:199). This is all fun stuff, but the laughter is to shake the reader out the dehumanizing habit shared by both scholars and romance writers alike who figure ancient Egyptians as an exotically foreign species. Chesterton urges a countervailing view of history that is a complement to the ethic of 'universal brotherhood' found in his fiction: he would 'really remind us that the ancient Egyptians were human beings'.

It is helpful at this point to return once more to James's lecture, to examine the *reason* he gives for why neutrality and objectivity are impossible. His explanation is simple, contentious and intuitively right: that neutral, objective reasoning is not the most powerful impulse determining a person's (even a philosopher's) view of the universe. 'The history of philosophy is', he says, 'to a great extent that of a certain clash of human temperaments': 'Undignified as such a treatment may seem to some of my colleagues, I shall have to take account of this clash and explain a good many of the divergencies of philosophers by it.'[5] Compare this to Chesterton's rationale for his 'sketch of religious history' in *The Everlasting Man*:

> ...with all decent deference to men much more learned than myself, I propose to cut across and disregard this modem method of classification, which I feel sure has falsified the facts of history. I shall here submit an alternative classification of religion or religions, which I believe would be found to cover all the facts and what is quite as important here, all the fancies. Instead of dividing religion geographically and as it were vertically, into Christian, Moslem, Brahmin, Buddhist, and so on, I would divide it psychologically and in some sense horizontally, into the strata of spiritual elements and influences that could sometimes exist in the same country, or even in the same man. (CW 2:219)

The continuity between James's principle and Chesterton's praxis is striking. James's account of the philosophical temperament cuts deeper, as he elaborates his argument:

> Of whatever temperament a professional philosopher is, he tries when philosophizing to sink the fact of his temperament. Temperament is no conventionally recognized reason, so he urges impersonal reasons only for his conclusions. Yet his temperament really gives him a stronger bias than any of his more strictly objective premises. It loads the evidence for him one way or the other, making for a more sentimental or a more hard-hearted view of the universe, just as this fact or that principle would. He trusts his temperament. Wanting a universe that suits it, he believes in any representation of the universe that does suit it. He feels men of opposite temper to be out of key with the world's character, and in his heart considers them incompetent and 'not in it,' in the philosophic business, even tho they may far excel him in dialectical ability.[6]

However far-reaching a critique of philosophical argument in general, its importance as applied to Chesterton can hardly be overstated: he cannot be at all understood until it is understood how thoroughly his philosophical approach to the universe is governed by how he *feels* about it. This goes beyond taking a special interest in a 'subjective history' that makes it 'an excellent habit to read history backwards' (CW 20:472). The importance of Chesterton's feeling about feeling goes beyond his belief that the atmosphere of an event can be more pertinent than the event itself. Chesterton did not believe there was anything worth thinking about that could be known in objective terms; he describes 'reason' as 'itself a matter of faith': 'It is an act of faith to assert that our thoughts have any relation to reality at all' (CW 1:236). As such, in an unembarrassed way, his subjectivity informs the way in which he interprets everything: the facts, their perception and the relationship between them. He was mindful of the psychological divisions that separate people and periods, but it is no less important to notice the character of his own overwhelming temperamental bias that (in everything of which he was and was not aware) 'loads the evidence for him'.

In his introduction to a new edition of *A Short History of England*, Chesterton reviews what he has learned since its first publication: 'Everything', he swells, 'has led me to think I was much more right than I thought I was': 'Such amateur history must be a little like guesswork; but I have almost a retrospective shiver at my own good luck in having so often guessed right.' What he calls guesswork is, more accurately, inference from fixed assumptions and limited facts. The facts are not decisive one way or another; there is no definitive empirical evidence: but Chesterton draws his conclusions with no less confidence, because he trusts his view of the universe; because, above all – as James would have it – he trusts his temperament. How does he know materialism is 'like the lucid scheme of the madman'? Simply, because its lucidity is schematic: 'it is not thinking of the real things of the earth, of fighting peoples or proud mothers, or first love or fear upon the sea' (CW 1:225). What a devastating little list that is. And what a perfect, perfectly Chestertonian touch to have 'proud mothers' nestle beside 'fighting peoples' in this confounding affirmation of life as *lived*.

A reviewer of *Heretics* in 1905 judged that Chesterton 'jumps rapidly to theories, and afterwards sets to thinking how best to make facts square with them' (CJ 105). This is almost, but not quite, fair comment. *Heretics* and its more thorough-going companion piece, *Orthodoxy*, proceed 'in a vague and personal way'; the latter attempts 'to state the philosophy' in which he has come to believe; it 'is not an ecclesiastical treatise but a sort of slovenly biography' (*CW* 1:211;215). With varying degrees of explicitness he acknowledges that he can do no more, because the quarrel is not, in the end, intellectual, it is temperamental; it is not about the facts, it is about how the facts make a person feel.[7] 'If I gave each of my reasons for being a Christian', he elsewhere observes, 'a vast number of them would be Mr. Blatchford's reasons for not being one'.[8] 'At a very early age', he explains in his *Autobiography*, 'I had thought my way back to thought itself. It was a very dreadful thing to do; for it may lead to thinking that there is nothing but thought' (*CW* 16:95). In other words, his faith only comes to him once he came to have faith in faith itself. Before he had religious belief, he 'believed in what some have called "the wish to believe"' (*CW* 16:159).

Whereas feeling and faith are epistemological bedfellows – religious conviction is not reached by rationality alone – there is no equivalent affinity between personal feelings and historical facts. For this reason, amongst all the genres of his writing, the essential subjectivity in his work operates most powerfully in his histories. But to appreciate what this means elucidates more than his histories. The trust he puts in his temperament explains his whole view of the universe.

James regrets that in defining philosophical positions, 'the potentest of all our premises is never mentioned'.[9] But Chesterton mentions it constantly. His biographies are a taxonomy of temperaments. One type he finds in, say, Blake's 'abrupt innocence' (*WB* 8), and in 'Browning's optimism' (*RB* 181). Another, in 'the most restless and incalculable' behaviour of Cobbett (*WC* 47), and a 'certain precipitancy' in St Francis that 'was the very poise of his soul' (*CW* 2:49). Another still, in the suspicion that 'there was something elvish' about Chaucer's mind (*CW* 18:165), and the satisfaction at Dickens's propensity to 'make men feel that this dull middle class was actually a kind of Elfland' (*CW* 15:77). He identifies many more shades. The common theme (as suggested in the previous chapter) is that the individual temperament must in the end be read *against* their environment, a people *against* their period; his sketches are the 'decisive curves and angles determined by the will of man'. 'The materialist theory of history, that all politics and ethics are the expression of economics, is', he insists, 'a very simple fallacy indeed': 'It consists simply of confusing the necessary conditions of life with the normal preoccupations of life, that are quite a different thing':

> It will be hard to maintain that the Crusaders went from their homes into a howling wilderness because cows go from a wilderness to a more comfortable grazing-ground. It will be hard to maintain that the Arctic explorers went north with the same material motive that made the swallows go south. (CW 2:269)

But there is 'a deeper fallacy':

> The truth is that the thing most present to the mind of man is not the economic machinery necessary to his existence; but rather that existence itself; the world which he sees when he wakes every morning and the nature of his general position in it. There is something that is nearer to him than livelihood, and that is life...Even those dry pedants who think that ethics depend on economics must admit that economics depend on existence...They all come back to what a man fundamentally feels, when he looks forth from those strange windows which we call the eyes, upon that strange vision that we call the world. (CW 2:270)

If what is most present to the mind of man is existence itself, life, feeling, Chesterton believes as strongly that men exist, live, feel, differently according to their own temperaments – even if unbeknown to them. The following excerpt is the last few sentences from a chapter entitled, 'The Philosophy of Gesture' in his biography of Stevenson; he has just described the 'tendency' of the age in which Stevenson lived:

> Stevenson felt all this, without exactly defining it; he felt it in the realism of nineteenth-century literature, in the pessimism of contemporary poetry, in the timidity of hygienic precaution, in the smugness of middle-class uniformity. And while he was entirely of that time and society, while he read all the realists, knew all the artists, doubted with the doubters and even denied with the deniers, he had that within him which could not but break out in a sort of passionate protest for more personal and poetical things. He flung out his arms with a wide and blind gesture, as one who would find wings at the moment when the world sank beneath him. (CW 18:130–1)

That double negative, 'could not but break out', is beautifully done: it catches precisely that never-mentioned potentest of all our premises. Chesterton reacts so strongly towards Stevenson because he is saluting a kindred temperament. He is moved to observe that, in contrast to Stevenson's fiction, the 'characteristic contemporary literature' displays 'an almost complete absence of joy. And I think it would be true to say, in a general fashion, that it is not childish enough to be cheerful' (CW 18:141). T. S. Eliot is impatient with such 'outbursts of heavy-weight Peter-Pantheism'. Chesterton's 'fashion' is, he says, '*too* general' (CJ 445). Perhaps it is. But perhaps Chesterton even knew that it was: the man who 'will generally be found restoring the world to sanity by exaggerating whatever the world neglects' is, he elsewhere suggests, the very definition of the saint (CW 2:424). The quibble is not in any case a question of exaggeration; it is not a matter of emphasis. What separates Chesterton's view of the universe from that of Eliot as expressed in his modernism-defining poem is a difference in kind. It is difference in temperament. For Chesterton, only the modern assumption that we are living in a waste land inhibits our wonder. Years before Eliot levied his criticism, Chesterton made clear his view that 'Peter Pan does not belong to the world of Pan but to the world of Peter' (CW 2:332).

Chesterton never lost this youthful optimism, which he redirected in his later years away from the legacy of late-Victorian decadence to the self-described despair of modernism. It is not that he thinks this the best of all possible worlds; he is an 'optimist' in thinking this is 'certainly not the best of all possible worlds, but it is the best of all possible things that a world should be possible' (GW 146). The reason he never lost his sense of wonder was because that sense was ineliminably part of who he was. Read back into the quotation on Stevenson. Substitute 'Stevenson' for 'Chesterton'; then consider the 'tendency' of the age in which Chesterton lived; consider what he felt but could not at first exactly define. Only once this has been done is it possible to approximate the import of his passionate protests that he could not but express. It is not to belittle the subtlety of Chesterton's thinking or his commitment to his creed to see that his, too, is, ultimately, a philosophy of gesture.[10]

Chesterton died in 1936. It was the same year his *Autobiography* appeared. It was also the same year in which George Orwell published *Keep the Aspidistra Flying*. Comparing these books provides a neat clarification of Chesterton's counter-cultural position. He was by no means blind to that 'sick cloud upon the soul' of modern man.[11] But whereas this leads many prominent intellectuals and artists of the early twentieth century to lugubrious lucubrations, and a defensive faith in (what D. H. Lawrence called) the necessity of a 'body of esoteric doctrine, defended from the herd',[12] Chesterton asserts the redemptive, and accessible appreciation of beauty in everyday life and in a thoroughly democratized art. Here is Orwell's expression of modernist alienation and anomie, through the character of Gordon Comstock:

> My poems are dead because I'm dead. You're dead. We're all dead. Dead people in a dead world... This life we live nowadays! It's not life, it's stagnation, death-in-life. Look at all these bloody houses, and the meaningless people inside them! Sometimes I think we're all corpses. Just rotting upright.[13]

How different is Chesterton's coeval judgement on how 'the modern mode of life, only professing to be prosaic, pressed upon' working men and women 'day and night', and that this 'was the real moulder of their minds' (CW 16:132). Whereas Comstock falls from idealism into cynicism, from optimism to pessimism, Chesterton records how he 'always retained a dim sense of something sacred' that separated him from 'the pessimism of the period'. He never comes to see meaningless people rotting upright in their houses: 'I never doubted that the human beings inside the houses were themselves almost miraculous; like magic and talismanic dolls' (CW 16:135).

The aesthetics of wonder is an older, different thing from the philosophy that inspires, and is inspired by, the aesthetics of the sublime. Given the timing of his birth, Chesterton ought to have been the inheritor of high Romanticism and the 'spilt religion' of Kant and Burke. But he is less interested in fear than in surprise. And his subjectivity services more than a secular enlightenment sense of self. The delightful wonder of life is everywhere apparent to him; and the causes of wonder are as modest as his joy is, literally, outlandish; as of a foreigner who lavishes praise on that which is seen for the first time. He asks 'through what incarnations or pre-natal purgatories' he must have passed 'to gain the reward of looking at a dandelion'. What he says about the dandelion applies equally to 'the sunflower or the sun, or the glory which (as the poet said) is brighter than the sun': namely, that 'the only way to enjoy' life and the world is 'to feel unworthy even of a weed' (CW 16:321). For him, 'thanks are the highest form of thought', and 'gratitude is happiness doubled by wonder' (CW 20:463).

Chesterton had so much to tell his contemporaries about *What's Wrong With the World* for the same reason he still has so much to tell. The problems with which he wrangled were to some extent particular to his time, but his solutions are more than reactionary: they derive from principles that touch his temperament and transcend his moment. He thought it a 'high boast' to be 'a medievalist and not a modern' (*AD* 7).[14] Just as Thackeray was 'too Victorian to understand the Victorian epoch' (CW 15:476), Chesterton was able to understand his own epoch for being little enough in it; or rather, enough out of it. The point may be extended to say that where he read history so well, he did so because he was so unconstrained by the prejudices of the present.[15]

There has been a tendency to equate Chesterton's philosophical temperament with his Catholicism. There is some sense in this. He emphasizes at every opportunity that his conversion was not from one set of assumptions to another wholly different set of assumptions, it was the ratification of his first assumptions. 'When I fancied that I stood alone', he explains, 'I was really in the ridiculous position of being backed up by all Christendom . . . I did try to be original; but I only succeeded in inventing all by myself an inferior copy of the existing traditions of civilized religion' (CW 1:214). Readers may be more or less satisfied with this testimony, and with the attempts by subsequent (inevitably Catholic) critics to show that although he did not convert until 1922, he was a robust defender of Catholic orthodoxy at least fifteen years earlier. But the important point being made here is a different one. What is being asserted here is that however much he may have been, down to the papal letter, a Catholic before he knew it himself, when he does find Catholicism, what he finds is something he *feels* to be right. He discovers religious expression for that something within him which 'could not but break out'.

What eventually breaks out into Catholicism is nonetheless more elusive than any creed, and more vital than any dogma. What he was before and after his conversion was, in his own terms, an 'optimist'. He happened to find in his faith an infinitely rich and stimulating expression of this temperamental bias, which subsequently inflected his political commentary (on everything from militarism to Distributism). But he also brought to his Catholicism something more than mere optimism, and to his politics something more than his religion. As ever, the best description of Chesterton may be found in his own words, written about someone else. The following, passing remark on Robert Browning is as good as any single sentence gloss could be for Chesterton's 'view of the universe'. Notice how the observation is cast in the present tense, giving a grammatical accent to the appreciation of one whose significance remains immediate, of one who still lives, vividly, in his writing; how aptly that redounds. Senescence never curbed his griggish gratitude for existence itself; history for him occurs in the now, and the joy undimmed in his lifetime reads brightly still, in ours. 'He is something far more convincing, far more comforting, far more religiously significant than an optimist: he is a happy man' (*RB* 186).

Notes

INTRODUCTION

1. Reported by T. E. Lawrence, quoted in M. Ward, *G. K. Chesterton* (London: Sheed and Ward, 1944), 313. Chesterton once quipped that his weight had never been 'successfully calculated' (as a young man he was actually very slim); and reports of his height vary too (he described himself as 'about six-foot two', whereas Dorothy Collins put him a good two inches taller). His actual dimensions are, however, less relevant than the extent to which his personality and physical presence seemingly *combined* to grant him improbable proportions. Shaw wrote of him in 1906: 'Chesterton is our "Quinbus Flestrin", the young Man Mountain, a large abounding gigantically cherubic person who is not only large in body and mind beyond all decency, but seems to be growing larger as you look at him...' (Ibid. 139).
2. *Occasional Sermons*, ed. Philip Caraman, (London, Burns & Oates [c.1960]), 402–5 (402).
3. Ibid. 402.
4. Aidan Nichols, for instance, quotes this comment from Chesterton's book *The Victorian Age in Literature* as being of unquestionable 'prophetic' value in *G. K. Chesterton, Theologian* (London: Darton, Longman and Todd, 2009), xviii. Debates on Chesterton as mystic typically emphasize what Bob Wild calls his 'charism of truth', which, in the words of Cardinal Carter of Toronto, amounts to a 'truly prophetic gift' (see *The Holiness of G. K. Chesterton*, ed. William Oddie, (Herefordshire: Gracewing, 2010), 90–1).
5. *The Complete Sherlock Holmes* (Harmondsworth: Penguin, 1981): 'You know my method. It is founded upon the observation of trifles' (*The Boscombe Valley Mystery*, 214); 'It is, of course, a trifle, but there is nothing so important as trifles' (*The Man with the Twisted Lip*, 238); 'It has long been an axiom of mine that the little things are infinitely more important' (*A Case of Identity*, 194); '"I am glad of all details,"' remarked my friend, "whether they seem to you to be relevant or

not'" (*The Copper Beeches*, 324); and so on.

6. Editorial Introduction, *The Club of Queer Trades* (Wordsworth Classics, 1995).

7. 'Art as Technique', in *Literary Theory: An Anthology* ed. Julie Rivkin and Michael Ryan. (Malden: Blackwell Publishing Ltd, 1998), 19.

8. Although his phrase-making is extraordinarily original, he often recycles his favourite figures: this one appears in modulated form in his biography of Cobbett: 'But even so there would only have been found, like some strange sunrise under the sea, under his all too salt humour and all the waters of bitterness that had gone over him, a lucid and enduring surprise' (*WC* 139).

9. This motif recurs throughout Chesterton's writing; as in, for instance, his essay 'On Mammoth Portraiture', where, surveying the schemes, systems and practical institutions of the modern living world, he concludes: 'We have lost the power to control things largely because we have lost the power to oversee them; that is, to see them as a whole' (*AS* 20).

10. Inexplicably, the text given in the *Collected Works* omits the paragraph from which I am quoting: my reference may be taken from the Hodder and Stoughton edition (1947), 20.

11. *The Tablet*, 20 June, 1936, 785. This quotation is taken from a longer passage cited by Ian Boyd in *The Novels of G. K. Chesterton* (London: Elek, 1975), 2. Boyd offers a lucid account of how critics have divided Chesterton's writings into 'art' and 'propaganda', and why this division is inadequate in respect of Chesterton's fiction.

12. *The Novels of G. K. Chesterton*, 3–5.

13. *TLS*, 28 Jan 2009.

14. 'Philosophy (the love of wisdom) arose then, as it still arises from wonder...a man labouring under astonishment and perplexity is conscious of his own ignorance...and if men philosophized in order to escape from ignorance, they were evidently in search of knowledge for its own sake and not for any practical results that might derive from it.' See an excellent treatment of this quotation in Pat Boyde's chapter, 'Wonder and Knowledge', in *Dante Philomythes and Philosopher* (Cambridge: CUP, 1981), Ch. 2. Philip Fisher makes the point that 'admiration' in its root 'mira', is both the Latin for 'wonder' and also the root word for 'miracle' in *Wonder, The Rainbow, and the Aesthetics of Rare Experiences* (Cambridge, Mass., and London, England: Harvard University Press, 1998), 11.

15. Quoted in Michael Coren, *Gilbert: the Man Who Was Chesterton* (London: Jonathan Cape, 1989), 62.

16. *Occasional Sermons*, 403.

17. '[T]he thing [Blake] hated most about art was the thing which we now call Impressionism – the substitution of atmosphere for shape,

the sacrifice of form to tint, the cloudland of the mere colourist' (*BK* 17–18).

18. *Seven Types of Ambiguity* 3rd edn. (London: Penguin, 1995), 36–7.
19. Lawrence J. Clipper, *G. K. Chesterton* (New York: Twayne Publishers, 1974), Preface.
20. Ian Crowther's admirable introduction is limited precisely by its method of presenting the 'vision which animated just about everything that Chesterton did and wrote' without adequate consideration of *how* he wrote, in *G. K. Chesterton* (London: Claridge Press, 1991), 7.
21. Quentin Lauer's otherwise excellent study exemplifies this tendency: *G. K. Chesterton: Philosopher Without Portfolio* (Fordham University Press, 1988), 8–9.
22. *G. K. Chesterton, Theologian*, xiv. Nichols has a keen sense of how Chesterton 'belongs to the tradition of philosophy, stretching from Plato to Kierkegaard, which regards rhetoric as a necessary concomitant of argument' (114); how Chesterton 'sought to practice metaphysics through a synthesis of philosophy and mythopoetic thought' (85); and how, for him, 'the Incarnation of the Word makes possible precisely such a union' (85). It is all finely done, so far as it goes; but this present study aims to show that the 'union' extends much further. To show why his overtly philosophical works must be read more thoroughly for their (mytho-)poetry; but also, why his creative writing offers unique, complementary and corrective accounts of his thinking.
23. P. N. Furbank, for instance, identifies this phrase as a 'central belief' in Chesterton ('Chesterton the Edwardian', in J. Sullivan (ed.) *G. K. Chesterton: A Centenary Appraisal* (London, 1974, 21–2); and yet, he does not pause to consider what, precisely, in its slippery literariness, this 'belief' might be. Oddie and Nichols (to give just two more examples) both likewise present the phrase as if its implications were not only central to Chesterton's thinking but also self-evident (see, respectively, *The Holiness of G. K. Chesterton*, 13: *G. K. Chesterton, Theologian*, 113–14).
24. See Christopher Ricks's analysis of Hamlet's line, as against Milton's 'successful' and 'unsuccessful' metaphors: *Milton's Grand Style* (Oxford: Clarendon Press, 1985), 50.
25. *Men in Dark Times* (London: Jonathan Cape, 1970), 155–6.

1. FICTION

1. *Aspects of the Novel* (London: Hodder and Stoughton, 1993), 46–54 (46–7).

2. Ibid. 49.
3. Ibid. 50.
4. *The Complete Sherlock Holmes*, 470–71.
5. (*TT* 178); the essay ('Some Policemen And A Moral') continues: This 'perennial temptation to a shameful admiration, must, and, I think, does, constantly come in and distort and poison our police methods'; 'If a man wished to hear the worst and wickedest thing in England summed up in casual English words, he would not find it in any foul oaths or ribald quarrelling. He would find it in the fact that the best kind of working man, when he wishes to praise any one, calls him "a gentleman". It never occurs to him that he might as well call him "a marquis", or "a privy councillor" – that he is simply naming a rank or class, not a phrase for a good man.'
6. Whereas, he thought, Dickens was a supremely democratic writer in the way he showed all men delightfully interesting in their diversity, Scott shows the concealed sublimity and dignity of every separate man (*CW* 15:178–81).
7. 'On Chesterton', in *Other Inquisitions 1937–1952*, trans. by Ruth L. C. Simms (Austin: University of Texas Press, c.1964), 84; 82.
8. 'Gothic' can mean several things: it is taken here in the rather baggy way that Chesterton often did, for the 'atmospheric' overlap – aesthetic and ideological – it suggests between a style of architecture and the grotesque horrors associated with the Gothic novel.
9. William Oddie, *Chesterton and the Romance of Orthodoxy* (Oxford: OUP, 2008), 332.
10. *TLS*, 30 July, 2010 (5). For a different and more thorough-going exploration of how, *contra* Wilson, concepts of evil are at the centre of Chesterton's thinking and writing, see Mark Knight, *Chesterton and Evil* (NY: Fordham University Press, 2004).
11. Evangelical atheist Slavoj Žižek, for instance, reads the climax of *The Man Who Was Thursday* as expressing 'the fundamental insight of Orthodoxy' (*The Monstrosity of Christ*, 48).
12. Henri de Lubac, *Catholicism: Christ and the Common Destiny of Man* (Tunbridge Wells: Burns and Oates Ltd., 1950), 31. And elsewhere: 'Catholicism is essentially social. It is social in the deepest sense of the word: not merely in its applications in the field of natural institutions but first and foremost in itself, in the heart of its mystery, in the essence of its dogma. It is social in a sense which should have made the expression "social Catholicism" pleonastic' (15).
13. Chesterton railed against the Mental Deficiency Act, which he considered to be 'the first eugenics law' (see Ian Ker, *G.K. Chesterton: A Biography* (Oxford: OUP, 2011), 462). Ker also makes the valuable

observation that, much as Father Brown solves crime through a reflexive sense of his own capacity for sin, Gabriel Gale, the poet in *The Poet and the Lunatics*, is able to see sense in the purportedly mad characters with whom he deals because he too has 'a streak...of the moonshine that leads men astray' (597).

14. 'How to Write a Detective Story', *G. K.'s Weekly*, 17 Oct 1925. For an elaboration on Chesterton's ideas on how the 'true object' of the mystery tale is not to mystify, but to 'enlighten', see my introduction to the Penguin Classics edition of *The Complete Father Brown Stories* (2012).

2. POETRY

1. *Seven Types*, 48.
2. *T. S. Eliot, Selected Prose* ed. John Hayward (London: Penguin, 1953), 118.
3. *A Choice of Kipling's Verse made by T. S. Eliot* (London: Faber and Faber, 1942), 6.
4. Ibid., 13.
5. For instance: the last line of stanza 30, section VI: 'Belief that grew of all beliefs/ One moment back was blown/ And belief that stood on unbelief/ Stood up iron and alone.'
6. For instance: stanza 48, section VII: 'Barriers go backwards, banners rend,/ Great shields groan like a gong–/ Horses like horns of nightmare/ Neigh horribly and long.'
7. Recall also his comments on *The Ball and the Cross*, considered in the previous chapter; or read his life of St Francis, where he denies that there is, 'as pacifists and prigs imagine, the least inconsistency between loving men and fighting them, if we fight them fairly and for good cause' (*CW* 2:53).
8. Of the many uses and abuses to which Chesterton has been put, he has been made a mouthpiece for the defenders of Englishness in almost every form: from those seeking to protect the English countryside, to those promoting a racist political agenda in the name of nationalism. It is easy to see how the often-quoted first couplet of 'The Secret People' offers just the right tone for both the liberal but trenchant, and also the bigoted and threatening: 'Smile at us, pay us, pass us; but do not quite forget,/ For we are the people of England, that never has spoken yet.' See Patrick Wright's article 'After Identity', in *Race, Identity and Belonging: a Soundings collection*, eds. Sally Davidson and Jonathan Rutherford (London: Lawrence and Wishart, 2008).

9. Abbott, C. C. (ed.), *The Letters of Gerard Manley Hopkins to Robert Bridges*. 2nd imp. rev. (London: OUP, 1955), 304.
10. Note to the second edition of 'The Wild Knight' (*CP* 318).
11. E. J. West (ed.), *Shaw on Theatre* (New York, 1961), 161.
12. The defining atmosphere of the novel is that of the fairytale (as Chesterton was to say of Dickens's stories) whose lightness lifts it up to our mythic imagination. As a play, where the action is performed in real time by real men, it risks appearing, at best, slapstick – which pulls the story *down*, for belly-laughs.

3. ESSAYS

1. Quoted by W. H. Auden (*HC* 263).
2. It is instructive to compare Chesterton's views on the essay form with those Theodor W. Adorno expresses a couple of decades later in 'Der Essay als Form' (*Notes to literature* ed. Rolf Tiedemann; trans. by Shierry Weber Nicholsen (New York: Columbia University Press, *c.* 1991–2). Consider in particular Adorno's conviction that 'Luck and play are essential' to the essay form (4), that it 'does not let its domain be prescribed for it' (4); and that it 'does not aim at a closed deductive or inductive structure' (10); that it 'uses equivocations not out of sloppiness, nor in ignorance of the scientific ban on them ... but to make it clear that when a word covers different things they are not completely different' (22), and that – in terms that would especially appeal to Chesterton – 'the essay's innermost formal law is heresy. Through violations of the orthodoxy of thought, something in the object becomes visible which it is orthodoxy's secret and objective aim to keep invisible' (23). Also pertinent are his cultural observations on why the essayist is popularly figured as 'one who squanders his intelligence in impotent speculation' (4), and that to praise someone as an essayist 'is enough to keep him out of academia' (3).
3. 'The Essay', *Essays of the Year: 1931–32* (London: The Argonaut Press, 1932), xiii. Correspondingly, his fear for the essay is that it will become 'more cogent and dogmatic' (xvii).
4. Coleridge perhaps offers a helpful hint here, when in describing the process of the 'imagination' he has us consider what it is we actually do when we 'leap': 'We first resist the gravitating power by an act purely voluntary, and then by another act, voluntary in part, we yield to it in order to alight on the spot, which we had previously proposed to ourselves'; like 'a small water-insect', we win our way up against the stream 'by alternate pulses of active and passive motion, now resisting the current, and now yielding to it in

order to gather strength and a momentary fulcrum for a further propulsion': *The Collected Works of Samuel Taylor Coleridge, Biographia Literaria* eds. James Engell and W. Jackson Bate (Princeton, NJ: Princeton UP, 1983), 124. To miss this double movement in the argumentation of Chesterton's essays neglects not only his 'passive motion', it misunderstands why but also how he is 'active'.

5. See, also, Nichols's argument that 'surprise' is, for Chesterton, the 'conceptual link' between 'joy' and 'gift' (*Chesterton, Theologian*, 115–16).

6. There would be no contradiction here for Chesterton, who described the Catholic Church as 'the one supremely inspiring and irritating institution in the world' (*CW* 3:385–6).

7. *Essays of the Year*, xiii.

8. Ibid. xiv.

9. (*CW* 4:209). Chesterton's sensitivity to the way in which metaphors shape ideas sees him argue in the opposite way too. The first essay in *What's Wrong With the World* begins by exposing 'one of the fifty fallacies that comes from the modern madness for biological or bodily metaphors' that has produced the gaping absurdity of perpetually talking about 'young nations' and 'dying nations', as if a nation had a fixed and physical span of life (*CW* 4: 39).

10. Y. Denis, *G. K. Chesterton: Paradoxe et Catholicisme*, 155.

11. *Chesterton, Theologian*, 101.

12. *Further Paradoxes*, trans. by Ernest Beaumont (London: Longmans, Green; Westminster, Md.: Newman Press, *c.*1958), 11.

13. Ibid. 9–10.

14. *Monstrosity of Christ*, 44.

15. Ibid. 73.

16. *Further Paradoxes*, 9–10.

17. Ibid. 14.

18. Compare Adorno's account of how all 'concepts' in the essay 'are to be presented in such a way that they support one another, that each becomes articulated through its configuration with the others . . . discrete elements set off against one another come together to form a readable context; the essay erects no scaffolding and no structure. But the elements crystallize as a configuration through their motion. The constellation is a force field, just as every intellectual structure is necessarily transformed into a force field under the essay's gaze' (*Notes to literature*, 13).

19. For an account of Ruskin's fall, see my essay, 'On or about July 1877', in *Victorian Transformations: Genre, Nationalism, and Desire in Nineteenth-Century Literature* ed. Bianca Tredennick (Ashgate, 2011).

4. BIOGRAPHY

1. He had a particular animus against Hardy (lashing into him elsewhere too); seventeen years after this much-quoted comment, however, his view seems to have become rather more sympathetic (*CI* 129).
2. Critics have been slow to take the hint. More than six decades later, William B. Furlong argues for the importance of his comparative study with the complaint that 'so little has been written about' the relationship between these men who were 'admired by their contemporaries as giants' in *GBS/GKC: Shaw and Chesterton: The Metaphysical Jesters* (University Park: Pennsylvania State University Press, 1970), Preface. But then, Furlong misses the trick, by exaggerating how 'strikingly similar' are their writing styles, and how 'diametrically different' their beliefs (188).
3. Cecil Chesterton, *Gilbert K. Chesterton: A Criticism* (New York: John Lane Co., 1909), 79.
4. Speculation over Shakespeare's faith is not itself a tedious undertaking; but Chesterton's amounts to mere assertion: 'That Shakespeare was a Catholic is a thing that every Catholic feels by every sort of convergent common sense to be true. It is supported by the few external and political facts we know; it is utterly unmistakeable in the general spirit and atmosphere' (*CW* 18:333).
5. *Margaret M. Morlier*, 'Sonnets from the Portuguese and the Politics of Rhyme, *Victorian Literature and Culture* (1999), 97–112; see also Sharon Smulders, "Medicated Music": Elizabeth Barrett Browning's Sonnets from the Portuguese', *Victorian Literature and Culture* 23 (1995), 193–213.
6. Oscar Wilde, 'The Critic as Artist,' in *Intentions* (London: Methuen, 1919; first pub. 1891), 201.
7. Maisie Ward quotes Chesterton's impenitent response: 'A wonderful instance of Dickens's never-varying propensity to keep ahead of his age' (*Chesterton*, 156).

5. HISTORY

1. *Pragmatism: A New Name For Some Old Ways of Thinking* (London: Longmans, Green & Co., 1907), 3.
2. John Dewey seemed to think so. But see Lee Oser's account of how Dewey may have 'missed Chesterton's [point] entirely': *The Return of Christian Humanism* (Columbia and London: University of Missouri Press, 2007), 28.

3. The *Collected Works* only publishes the original introduction to *A Short History of England*; this quotation comes from the more interesting introduction he wrote for a new edition of that book: see the Chatto and Windus text of 1930 (v).
4. Ibid. v.
5. *Pragmatism*, 6–7.
6. Ibid. 7.
7. Quoting David Fagerberg's observation that at the time of writing *Heretics* Chesterton was 'learning Christianity by a sort of *via negativa*', Nichols makes the astute, complementary observation that '*Orthodoxy* is the cataphatic completion, on a *via affirmativa* all Chesterton's own' (*Chesterton, Theologian*, 31).
8. 'Christianity and Rationalism', in *The Religious Doubts of Democracy*, ed. George Haw (London: Macmillan, 1904), 17–21 (18).
9. *Pragmatism*, 8.
10. Recall, by contrast, his cardinal criticism of Bernard Shaw quoted in the previous chapter: that 'He never breaks out into that cry beyond reason and conviction'. While Chesterton sometimes seems to allow only the binary alternatives of 'the Catholic religion' versus 'utter pessimistic scepticism' (CW 2:209–10), he does admit a sympathetic distinction between pessimism of 'The sad souls of the "nineties" who "lost hope because they had taken too much absinthe", and that of the "young men" scarred by war who "lost hope because a friend had died with a bullet in his head"' (quoted in Ker, *G. K. Chesterton*, 192).
11. This quotation comes from the second line of his epigraphic verses to *The Man Who Was Thursday*, noted in the first chapter.
12. James T. Boulton and Andrew Robertson (eds.), *The Letters of D. H. Lawrence, Vol. III, 1916–21* (CUP, 1984), 143. Lawrence's remark is quoted by John Carey in his *The Intellectuals and the Masses* (London: Faber and Faber, 1992), 71, a book which is at least as guilty of Eliot's criticism for being '*too* general' in his account of the bleak and bigoted outlook of the literary intelligentsia of the early twentieth century.
13. *The Complete Works of George Orwell*, Vol. 4 (London: Secker & Warburg, 1997), 92; 94.
14. Correspondingly, he elsewhere attacks 'the queer, automatic assumption that it must always mean throwing mud at a thing to call it a relic of medievalism' (AS 11).
15. The inverse also applies: the weakest part of his historical surveys is where he is most uncharacteristically of his moment. *A Short History of England* is 'so small a book on so large a matter, finished hastily enough amid the necessities of an enormous national crisis'; for this reason, he admits, 'it would be absurd to pretend to have achieved

proportion'. His is a concession to expediency: that he had not the space or the time to achieve the desired proportion. But the 'enormous national crisis' to which he refers – it was published in 1917 – distorts the book's narrative in a more direct way than he allows. It is perhaps sufficient to name the penultimate chapter – 'The Return of the Barbarian' – to suggest the way in which he sees the threat to England too presently to be able to view its history without foreshortening. Likewise, his thesis on Rome's perpetual resurrection – and his qualified admiration of Mussolini – makes *The Resurrection of Rome* very much a book written after the First World War, but before the Second.

Select Bibliography

WORKS BY CHESTERTON

The *Collected Works*, published by Ignatius Press, is a valuable and much overdue collection of all Chesterton's published work, including his previously uncollected journalism. Each edition comes with a helpful editorial introduction. The collection is not yet complete, and there are a few corruptions and omissions in certain published volumes. Nonetheless, this series will be the standard edition for many years to come. Otherwise, Penguin Classics are re-issuing *The Man Who Was Thursday* and *The Complete Father Brown Stories*. It is also worth noting that lovely early (though not necessarily first) editions can often be bought second-hand, and sometimes for cheaper than the cost of less handsome, recently re-printed volumes.

In addition to the specific scholarly works cited below, other important resources for anyone wanting to study Chesterton include: the extensive holdings of the British Library (including the Dorothy Collins papers, which may be searched in the *British Library Catalogue of Additions to Manuscripts*, (2001)); as well as journals such as *The Chesterton Review; Seven: An Anglo-American Literary Review*; and *English Literature in Transition*.

BIBLIOGRAPHY

Sprung, J. W. (ed.), *An Index to G. K. Chesterton* (Washington, 1966).
Sullivan, J. *G. K. Chesterton: a Bibliography, with an Essay on Books by G. K. Chesterton and an Epitaph by Walter de la Mare* (London, 1958).
———, *Chesterton Continued: A Bibliographical Supplement* (London, 1968).

BIOGRAPHY

Barker, D., *G. K. Chesterton* (London: Constable, 1973). Readable; shorter and more dispassionate than Maisie Ward's seminal work.
Coren, M., *Gilbert: The Man Who Was Chesterton* (London, 1989). A light but informative account that does well to bring him to life.
Dale, A. S., *The Outline of Sanity: A Biography of G. K. Chesterton* (Michigan: William B. Eerdmans Publishing Co., 1982). Contending that Chesterton's biographers have neglected to see him as a product of his times, this is an historical account of his 'rational balance' in an age of extremism.
Ffinch, Michael, *G. K. Chesterton* (London: Weidenfeld and Nicolson, 1986). Affectionate and thoroughly researched; takes as its chief concern the seeming paradox that 'in the cause of Liberty he also became a defender of the Faith'.
Ker, Ian, *G. K. Chesterton* (Oxford: OUP, 2011). More than seven hundred pages richly illustrated by quotations, this book presents much important new research but is expository rather than critically acute. It is thick with evidence that Chesterton believed humour to be inseparable from seriousness, and that 'limitation' may be liberating. Ker rates Chesterton's non-fiction far higher than his poems, plays or stories.
Oddie, William, *Chesterton and the Romance of Orthodoxy: the making of GKC, 1874–1908* (Oxford: OUP, 2008). Draws extensively on Chesterton's unpublished letters and notebooks, his journalism, and his early classic writings, to show that he was a trenchant defender of Roman Catholicism as much as fifteen years before his conversion.
Pearce, J., *Wisdom and Innocence: A Life of G. K. Chesterton* (London: Hodder & Stoughton 1996). Published on the 60th anniversary of his death and drawing on much previously unpublished material, this book looks to recuperate Chesterton's reputation by surveying the life and writing that once made him a household name.
Ward, Maisie, *Gilbert Keith Chesterton* (London: Sheed & Ward, 1944). This was the first major scholarly account of Chesterton's life, and still one of the most important.
——, *Return to Chesterton* (London: Sheed and Ward, 1952). No sooner had Ward finished her first biography than queries and quibbles from readers led her to produce this follow-up study.
Wills, Garry, *Chesterton* (2001). With only a new appendix and introduction, this book is the re-issue of *G. Chesterton: Man and Mask* (1961); Wills was allowed access to archival material (safe-guarded by Chesterton's former secretary, and literary executor,

Dorothy Collins) that was subsequently given to the British Library. An intelligent account of Chesterton's intellectual life that remains a valuable resource.

CRITICISM

Ahlquist, Dale, G. K. *Chesterton: The Apostle of Common Sense* (Ignatius Press, 2003). An accessible introductory survey of Chesterton's Christian works, illustrated by extensive quotations. Passionately asserts – rather than analytically demonstrates – its claim for Chesterton as 'the best writer of the twentieth century'.

Belloc, Hilaire, *On the place of Gilbert Chesterton in English letters* (London, Sheed & Ward, 1940). This book's principal (and not insignificant) interest lies in its being an intimate account of Chesterton by his most famous political partner.

Boyd, I., *The Novels of G. K. Chesterton* (London: Paul Elek, 1975). A lucid evaluation of eleven of Chesterton's novels; the book defines itself against the unhelpful critical custom of treating his writings as either 'art' or 'propaganda'.

Canovan, M., *G. K. Chesterton: Radical Popularist* (London: Harcourt Brace Jovanovich, 1977). Considering Chesterton's role as a free-floating intellectual outside of all political parties, this excellent book argues that although Chesterton's writings display the vices of populism, they also exemplify the significant virtues of the populist: respect for the humanity and dignity of ordinary people, and a refusal to be impressed by the claims of wealth and cleverness.

Chesterton, Cecil, *Gilbert K. Chesterton: A Criticism* (London: Alston Rivers, 1908). The obvious appeal of this account is that it is written by Gilbert's brother; Cecil is surprisingly hard (honest?) in his judgements.

Clemens, Cyril, *Chesterton as Seen by his Contemporaries* (Webster Groves, Mo.: International Mark Twain Society, 1939). A rich assembly of memories and appreciations collected under a variety of categories: shows the diverse attitude of his contemporaries better than any individual critic could describe it.

Clipper, L. J., *G. K. Chesterton* (New York: Twayne Publishers Inc., 1974). This book delineates Chesterton as 'a man of ideas'; he is not treated as an 'original thinker' but as a 'contemplative'.

Coates, J. D., *Chesterton and the Edwardian Cultural Crisis* (Hull, 1984). Provides a useful cultural context for his writing.

———, *G. K. Chesterton as Controversialist, Essayist, Novelist, and Critic* (Lewiston, NY: The Edwin Mellen Press, 2002). Attempts to show why Chesterton still matters today; again, valuable on the historical context.

Conlon, D. J. (ed.), *G. K. Chesterton: the critical judgements, 1900–1937* (Antwerp: Antwerp Studies in English Literature, 1976). An anthology of reviews offering a rich flavour of Chesterton's contemporary reception.

———, *G. K. Chesterton: A Half Century of Views* (Oxford: Oxford University Press, 1987). This follow-up anthology offers an instructive range of views on Chesterton's reception in the half century after his death.

Cooney, A., *G. K. Chesterton, One Sword at Least* (London: Third Way Publications, 1999). A pamphlet introduction that offers an interesting insight into his views on Distributism.

Corrin, Jay P., *G. K. Chesterton & Hilaire Belloc: the battle against modernity* (London: Ohio University Press, 1981). This book describes – often in their own words – the social and political side of the 'Chesterbelloc', the circle of writers who fought their cause, and the impact they had on British society.

Crowther, Ian, *G. K. Chesterton* (London: Claridge Press, 1991). A short, introductory study that aims to render Chesterton's thought intelligible to the modern reader.

Dale, Alzina Stone., *The Art of G. K. Chesterton* (Chicago: Loyola University Press, 1985). A selection of Chesterton's drawings and sketches annotated by a text that sets the biographical scene. It is no criticism of this text to say that the reader would like less of it, and more of Chesterton's art.

Denis, Y., *G. K. Chesterton: Paradoxe et Catholicisme* (Paris: Belles Lettres, 1978). A theological complement to and advance on Kenner's more philosophical account of *Paradox in Chesterton* (1948); subtle and well researched.

Dhar, Banshi, *G. K. Chesterton and the Twentieth-Century Essay* (New Delhi: S. Chand, 1977). This expanded doctoral thesis offers an assiduous survey of Chesterton's essays, which are contextualized in literary-historical terms, and evaluated under various categories, such as 'light', 'serious' and 'parables'.

Fagerberg, D. W., *The Size of Chesterton's Catholicism* (Notre Dame, Ind, and London: University of Notre Dame Press, 1998). Drawing on passages scattered throughout Chesterton's writings, this book explores how and why Chesterton insisted on the capacity and indeed the catholicity of his faith.

Furlong, William B., *GBS/GKC: Shaw and Chesterton: The Metaphysical Jesters* (University Park: Pennsylvania State University Press, 1970). A landmark comparative study that unfortunately exaggerates how 'strikingly similar' are their writing styles, and how 'diametrically different' their beliefs.

Hillier, Bevis, ed., *The Wit and Wisdom of G. K. Chesterton* (London and NY: Continuum, 2010). An attractive selection of Chesterton's most quotable quips, together with a sample of his pictures; prefaced by an astute introduction.

Hollis, Christopher, *The Mind of Chesterton* (London: Hollis & Carter, 1970). An intellectual biography (with an emphasis on his theology) that evaluates his relevance three decades after his death.

Hunter, Lynette., *G. K. Chesterton: explorations in allegory* (London: Macmillan, 1979). This is a subtle and thorough account of Chesterton as the 'mystic artist': of his allegorical attempts to build bridges between the human and the divine.

Jaki, S. L., *Chesterton, a Seer of Science* (Urbana: University of Illinois Press, c.1986). Unusual in Chesterton studies for shifting the claims for him as a thinker away from philosophy, theology and politics to his insights as 'Interpreter of Science', 'Antagonist of Scientism, 'Critic of Evolutionism' and 'Champion of the Universe'.

Ker, I., *The Catholic Revival in English Literature (1845–1961): Newman, Hopkins, Belloc, Chesterton, Greene, Waugh* (Indiana, Notre Dame: 2003). Beginning with Newman's conversion in 1845 and ending with Waugh's completion of *The Sword of Honour* trilogy in 1961, this book explores how Catholicism shaped the work of these six prominent writers.

Kenner, Hugh, *Paradox in Chesterton* (London: Sheed & Ward, 1948). The first sustained attempt to show that Chesterton was an important thinker. This present study objects to the founding premise of Kenner's thesis (that Chesterton's thinking and his writing can and should be separated). But that is not to deny the continuing value and relevance of Kenner's deeply intelligent contribution.

Knight, Mark, *Chesterton and Evil* (NY: Fordham University Press, 2004). This thoroughly researched book (its origin was as a PhD) variously challenges the popular but misguided idea of Chesterton as the naive optimist and argues instead that concepts of evil are at the centre of his thinking and writing.

Lauer, Quentin, *G. K. Chesterton: Philosopher Without Portfolio* (Fordham University Press, 1991). An important evaluation of Chesterton's philosophical thought, making a case first of all for him to be taken seriously as a philosopher, and then, as a thinker with thoughts relevant and pressing five decades after his death.

Macdonald, Michael H., *The Riddle of Joy: G. K. Chesterton and C. S. Lewis* (London: Collins, 1989). Seventeen essays collected under the categories of 'Riddling Remembrances from those who knew them', 'Spelling the riddle: Literary Assessments', 'Living the Riddle: Their Social thought', 'Proclaiming the Riddle: Their social thought' and 'Pursuing the Riddle of Joy'.

McCleary, Joseph R., *The Historical Imagination of G. K. Chesterton* (London: Routledge, 2009). Argues with great sophistication that the interlocking themes of locality, patriotism and nationalism constituted the essential elements of the philosophy of history that informed much of Chesterton's critical and literary work.

Milbank, Alison, *Chesterton and Tolkien as theologians: the fantasy of the real* (London: T & T Clark, c.2007). A convincing demonstration that as essayist, poet, Christian apologist and writer of fantastic tales Chesterton was an important influence both on Tolkien's fiction and his literary criticism of the fairy tale.

Nichols, Aidan, *G. K. Chesterton, Theologian* (London: Darton, Longman and Todd, 2009). This wonderfully authoritative account is perhaps the best single book on Chesterton's theology.

Oddie, William ed., *The Holiness of G. K. Chesterton* (Herefordshire: Gracewing, 2010). Seven essays responding to the increasngly popular idea that Chesterton should be canonized.

Oser, Lee, *The Return of Christian Humanism* (Columbia and London: University of Missouri Press, 2007). A trenchant comparative study of Chesterton, T. S. Eliot and Tolkien as embattled Christian Humanists who understood their art as an effort to affirm the relationship between religion and literature.

Paine, R., *The Universe and Mr. Chesterton* (Illinois: Sherwood Sugdon & Co., 1999). Identifies Chesterton's importance not in the originality of his thinking but in the value of his writing as a philosophical propaedeutic: he prepares us for 'the real philosophers'.

Peters, Thomas C., *The Christian Imagination: G.K. Chesterton on the Arts* (San Francisco: Ignatius Press, 2000). An accessible look at Chesterton's approach to art, adventure and play specifically in terms of his 'Christian imagination'.

Schwartz, A., *The Third Spring: G. K. Chesterton, Graham Greene, Christopher Dawson, and David Jones* (Washington: The Catholic University Press, 2005). A comparative study of the spiritual journeys, religious and cultural beliefs of these four adult converts to Catholicism, considered as part of a renascent Catholic culture within a post-Christian society.

Stapleton, Julia, *Christianity, Patriotism and Nationhood: The England of G. K. Chesterton* (Lanham MD: Lexington Books, 2009). Linking the concepts of patriotism, Christianity, and English national identity in Chesterton's journalistic writings, this book explores the English attachments that were central to his political and spiritual persona.

Sullivan, J. (ed.), *G. K. Chesterton: A Centenary Appraisal* (New York, 1974). A valuable array of responses collected under three categories: the 'achievement', the 'man' and the 'relevance'.

Index

Lightning Source UK Ltd.
Milton Keynes UK
UKOW050427270612

195104UK00001B/11/P